Business Co

CW00871899

A comprehensive guid
business communication skills, negotiation skills,
and to avoid barriers in internal and external
communication of your company.

By

Shane Castro

© Copyright 2020 by (Shane Castro) - All rights reserved.

This document is geared towards providing exact and reliable information in regards to the topic and issue covered. The publication is sold with the idea that the publisher is not required to render accounting, officially permitted, or otherwise, qualified services. If advice is necessary, legal or professional, a practiced individual in the profession should be ordered.

- From a Declaration of Principles which was accepted and approved equally by a Committee of the American Bar Association and a Committee of

Publishers and Associations.

In no way is it legal to reproduce, duplicate, or transmit any part of this document in either electronic means or in printed format. Recording of this publication is strictly prohibited and any storage of this document is not allowed unless with written permission from the publisher. All rights reserved.

The information provided herein is stated to be truthful and consistent, in that any liability, in terms of inattention or otherwise, by any usage or abuse of any policies, processes, or directions contained within is the solitary and utter responsibility of the recipient reader. Under no circumstances will any legal responsibility or blame be held against the publisher for any reparation, damages, or monetary loss due to the information herein, either directly or indirectly.

Respective authors own all copyrights not held by the publisher.

The information herein is offered for informational purposes solely, and is universal as so. The presentation of the information is without contract or any type of guarantee assurance.

The trademarks that are used are without any consent, and the publication of the trademark is without permission or backing by the trademark owner. All trademarks and brands within this book are for clarifying purposes only and are the owned by the owners themselves, not affiliated with this document.

Table of contents

INTRODUCTION 6

CHAPTER 1: EFFECTIVE BUSINESS COMMUNICATION 8

1.1 What is Business Communication? 9

1.2 Objectives of Business Communication 16

1.3 Importance of Business Communication 21

1.4 Steps to set up a Communication Process.................27

1.5 Impacts of Ineffective Communication......................31

CHAPTER 2: TYPES OF BUSINESS COMMUNICATION.36

2.1 Structure-Based Communication Styles....................37

2.2 Dependent on the Communication Medium 39

2.3 Based on Path Flow 52

CHAPTER 3: METHODS OF BUSINESS COMMUNICATION 61

3.1 Telephone Meetings..61

3.2 Video Conferencing 62

3.3 The Memos..66

3.4 The Letter...67

3.5 Email..70

3.6 The Texting 73

3.7 Face-to-Face Meetings 79

CHAPTER 4: BARRIERS IN EFFECTIVE BUSINESS COMMUNICATION 83

4.1Barriers in Communication Process 83

4.2 Steps to Overcome Barriers 92

CHAPTER 5: EFFECTIVE COMMUNICATION MEANS BUSINESS SUCCESS 105

5.1 Communication is Crucial for A Successful Business 105

CONCLUSION..113

Introduction

In this competitive world, effective communication is an important element in the success of a company. The process of exchanging information between workers inside and outside an organization is business communications. In order to accomplish corporate goals and be more consistent with the core principles of the company, good business communication is how workers and management communicate with each other. The main trait of good company creators is the ability to interact with people both within and outside the organization.

Good communication strengthens the ties between an organization and all its stakeholders and benefits businesses in many ways: better decision-making and quicker problem solving; earlier notification of potential problems; enhanced efficiency and steadier workflow; stronger corporate relationships; simpler and more persuasive marketing messages; improved professional images for all empirical. It improves employee productivity and reduces employee turnover.

It has different types depending upon medium: it can be verbal (oral, written) nonverbal, which includes facial expressions, body language, posture, environment, paralanguage, and silence. Depending upon the direction of flow: it can be vertical (from managers to subordinates), horizontal (between managers), upward (from subordinates to managers and higher executives), and downward. And depending on structure: it can be formal and informal. It can be external (between the organization and its environment like other businesses, clients, and tax authorities, or it can be internal (within the organization). Each has its own benefits and disadvantages.

Different methods can be used to transfer information; it can be telephonic communication, face to face video conferencing, email, letter, message, and memos. The selection of medium should be cost-effective and time-efficient. Medium selection greatly affects the effectiveness of the communication system and the efficiency of work. Companies can choose any medium which is most suitable for them depending upon their size. Big companies use three or four mediums at the same time. Before using any medium, a company should provide proper training to its employees about how to use any medium, what are the outcomes of mistakes, and all the nitty-gritty about the medium in order to make it a smooth process. As it is a continuous process, it should be checked frequently.

There are different types of barriers which affect the process of communication: noise, psychological barriers, organizational barriers, status barriers, mechanical barriers, personal barriers, time pressure, stressful working environment, listening barriers, etc. there are various strategies which you can implement to overcome these barriers to improve efficiency and productivity.

Technical people with strong communication skills benefit more, and they suffer from those who are poor communicators. The argument was emphatically made by William Schaffer, an international business development manager for the computer giant Sun Microsystems: "If there's one ability required for success in this industry, its communication."

You will gain a big advantage in your career if you learn to write well, speak well, listen well, and understand the best way to interact in different business contexts. In addition, since your communication plays a key role in efforts to enhance effectiveness, efficiency, responsiveness, and creativity, the performance of your business is influenced by your communication.

Chapter 1: Effective Business Communication

Communication is a key aspect for the success of any company. The process of transmitting information from one person to another, inside and outside the business context, is termed as 'Business Communication.' The word 'Business Communication' is derived from general communication, which is synonymous with business activities. In other words, contact for business-related activities between business parties or people is known as 'Business Communication.

Different scholars have provided different business communication meanings: Business Communication is described as a mechanism that is responsible for influencing change in the entire enterprise, according to Ricks and Grow.

According to W.H., business communication is the sharing of different business-related ideas, opinions, and news among the related parties,

Prof. J. Haste claimed that it is known as business communication when communication exists between either two or more business people for the purpose of efficient business organization and administration.

The way workers and management interact to accomplish organizational objectives are successful in business communication. By reducing errors, the aim is to enhance organizational performance. Different areas of business communication include advertisement, public relations, customer relations, organizational and interpersonal communication, etc.

1.1 What is Business Communication?

The term communication is originated from the Latin word communis, meaning common. Communication, therefore, means the sharing of common ideas. The meaning of communication in the dictionary is to convey or exchange data and share views.

It is a mechanism by which two or more individuals communicate or exchange thoughts and ideas with each other. In accordance with W. H. Newman, communication is an exchange of facts, ideas, opinions, or emotions between two or more people.

F. Summer: In order to receive the desired response from the receiver, communication is the process of transferring information and suggestions from one person to another or from one unit to another unit. Two or more individuals exchange thoughts and understanding among themselves through this process to achieve the desired effect on another person's behavior.

It is a two-way channel for the transmission of ideas, emotions, plans, orders, instructions, reports, and suggestions that affect the attitude towards the goals of an organization. The objective of the communicator is to convey without distortion the meanings or ideas. The success of the leader and the company relies on communication adequacy.

The managers are responsible for setting up and maintaining the channels by which they can convey their own policies and thinking to the subordinates and receive their responses and account of their problems.

In the following manner, Louis A. Allen defines communication: Communication is the sum total of all the things one individual does in the mind of another when he wants to create understanding.

It is a bridge with importance. It requires a process of telling, listening, and understanding that is systematic and continuous.

In this definition of communication, it covers two elements. Firstly there is something that is passed on, such as facts, emotions, opinions, etc. It means that if communication is to occur, there must be a receiver.

Second, in the communication phase, the concept emphasizes the understanding or perception aspect. It would be possible to share understanding only when the person to whom the message is sent understands in the same sense as the message sender wants him to understand.

Therefore, contact requires something more than just transmission or delivery of the message and actual reception of it. From the perspective of organizational effectiveness, the right interpretation and comprehension of the message are critical. The exact transmission and reception of it, and its proper interpretation, may be successful communication as well.

C. L. Bovee, J. and B., in their book "Business Communication Today, define communication as the method of sending and receiving messages. E. Schatzman writes Communication, however, is only effective when the message is understood and when it stimulates action or motivates the recipient to think in new ways.

Communication between individuals to convey their personal information, message, or thought is personal communication, but the exchange of business-related information, facts, and ideas can be called Business Communication. Business communication relates to communication-related to business practices, which involves supplying customers with goods and services in order to make a profit.

It is a mechanism by which information, facts, advice, decisions, etc. are distributed, sent, c among business-related individuals. Communica to a company's trade, regulation, finance, adr management, etc. can therefore be referred to a ...siness Communication.

A business enterprise's success is primarily dependent on effective communication. The barriers to achieving the goal of a business organization are eliminated through effective communication. Inadequate communication or communication failure may result in a company's loss of money, time, resources, opportunity, and even goodwill.

Any business enterprise, big or small, needs adequate communication for its life in this age of globalization. The efficiency of any business concern largely depends on effective communication.

Sending information regarding the product to the ultimate consumer is very important in this age of speed, complexity, and competition. It is impossible for them to make an association and buy the product unless they know about the business company's product. In this area, communication plays a critical role.

- **Elements of business communication:**

Six fundamental elements are involved in business communication. They are as following:

1. Message: This is the subject-matter transmitted or passed on to the other party or group of individuals by the sender. This may be a view, order, suggestion, mood, feeling, belief, etc.

2. Sender: He/she is the individual who intends to make contact to pass on data and understanding to another person.

eceiver: The receiver is the person for whom the message is designed is known as the recipient or communicator.

4. Channels: Information is transmitted via certain channels (such as radio, television, telephone, mail, e-mail, etc.) provided different variables; the media is selected by the sender.

5. Symbols: These are the actions, words, and signs that are passed on while communicating with the receiver used by the sender.

6. The feedback: Feedback takes place when the receiver acknowledges the sender's message and responds back to him/her. Communication without feedback is incomplete.

- **Business communication features:**

Business communication has certain characteristics or features that allow us to differentiate it from other interactions. To be business communication, contact must be:

1. Practical: Efficient business communication focuses on the practical aspect of the data that explains why, how, when, and similar questions. To eliminate time-wasting, it avoids impractical, imaginary, unnecessary, or repetitive information. It gives the receiver important information.

2. Factual: A business message generally contains facts and figures instead of an overall idea. Important date, place, time, etc. must be stated clearly in business communication.

3. Brief and clear: The language used in business communication must be simple, brief, clear, and without ambiguity. Usually, charts, photographs, diagrams, etc. are used to compress or explain the information.

4. Goal-oriented: A business relationship must have a clear purpose and must be properly organized in order to achieve the goal.

5. Persuasive: Interaction with the company also plays a convincing function. It persuades a person to perform his / her duties, a client to purchase a product or service, etc. The basic characteristics referred to above are related to the message or to the communication details.

There are certain other features in the method of business communication. These are:

1. An essential part of the management process:

Communication involves all activities in which the managers' thoughts, views, and decisions are communicated to the subordinates of various levels. It also includes the exchange between superiors and subordinates of information, views, opinions, and responses.

In this way, communication brings people into action, guides, and directs their actions, rules them, and coordinates them for the proper performance of their work. Via correspondence, a manager performs the management roles, and managerial positions become the co-ordination centers to collect information from different sources for transmission to appropriate points.

Thus, contact is part and parcel of the role of management and is thus an integral part of the process of management. That is why, according to Chester I. Bernard, "the first executive role is to establish and sustain a communication structure."

2. Two-way traffic:

Not only does communication mean its downward transition from superior to a subordinate, but it also requires both transmission and reception. So, a manager should know his reactions and responses when conveying some information. Otherwise, it would be inefficient to guide and direct managerial activities.

Therefore, a man should not only speak, inform, and order but also be able to listen, respond, and interpret. Therefore, communication demands two-way traffic from the executives to the workers and from the workers to the executives. It is not finished until the message has been fully understood by the recipient, and the sender becomes aware of its response.

3. Mutual understanding:

The basic aim of business communication is to bring about understanding in the organization between individuals. It is an essential element for human relationships to be formed. By developing a perfect understanding with subordinates, colleagues, and superiors in the company, a leader can lead, and a manager can direct effectively.

The higher the level of understanding of communication, the more likely it is that human activity will continue in the direction of achieving the goals.

4. Pervasive:

Business communication involves a wide variety of subjects and includes all functions, including acquisitions, manufacturing, distribution, financing, recruiting, compensation, dividends, market position, creativity, efficiency, etc. It also passes through all management stages, upward, downward, and sideways. Therefore, business communication is said to be a pervasive feature.

5. Continuous process:

Communication is an occurrence that is ever-present, and an organization does not survive without it. For an organization, communication is as vital as blood circulation in a living body. Managers should also ensure that information passes in all directions properly and smoothly.

Communication breakdown results in confusion, the emergence of adverse attitudes, hostility, and conflict. Thus, for the active involvement of those concerned, communication must be an ongoing process and travel up, down, and sideways.

6. Specifics:

Generally, business communication is unique in nature. This implies that a specific interaction should deal with a single subject at a time. For the efficiency of the communication process, this is important. The multiplicity of subjects in communication can generate confusion that is hazardous to crash management. With respect to the information or data intended to transmit or received, it must be specific.

7. Outcome and not cause:

The product of competent management, not the source of it, is sound communication. Business communication is an agent to an end and works in the hands of executives as a weapon. Effective management of this instrument depends on the abilities of the executives. It is not an autonomous task but an integral component of the executive function.

Therefore, outstanding communication does not produce a good boss. But a good director is almost always a good communicator. Misunderstanding of the process of management also leads to poor communication.

8. External and internal:

Communication with the company is mainly internal. It is, therefore, part of an administrative role and meant to be extended to members of an organization. Some examples of internal communication are directives, directions, recommendations, and even public announcements announcing the annual general meeting of a corporation.

But today, many interactions go beyond the corporate horizons and impact the outside population (e.g., advertising) that exceeds the organization's own. Accordingly, business communication can be internal and external.

9. Types different:

There may be various forms of business communication: formal, informal, upward, downward, sideways, written, oral, etc.

10. The feedback:

If and until the recipient's input or answer is given, correspondence will not be completed. Written, oral or gestural input can be included. Mere silence may also often constitute feedback.

1.2 Objectives of Business Communication

The primary objective of communication is to provide information and to convince different individuals. Other goals include the transmission of suggestions, opinions, ideas, advice, requests, etc.; instruction, guidance, and counseling; training; warning; appreciation of good work, moral enhancement, etc. The main objective of communication in the case of a business enterprise is the advancement of its activities, the overall development of the company, and the ultimate success in its functioning.

1. Information:

The primary objective of communication is to make an organization's members aware of its purpose and to familiarize them with all the important news. This helps the company to achieve success through coordinated efforts by all concerned individuals. It is a fact that it is possible for well-informed people to achieve better.

Managers should understand in detail the social, political, economic, and other circumstances of the place where the company is located. Data about workers, customers, and rivals must be at their fingertips. Employees should also be well-informed about their positions, powers, and duties in particular, and the organization's goals and objectives in general.

Information on the consumer's demand for a specific product, taste, liking, etc.; availability of raw materials, credit facilities, and advertising media; the production and sale of the product require the latest government rules and regulations, etc.

It is possible to obtain information from past records, books, journals, newspapers, publications of the government, seminars, conferences, exhibitions, trade fares, etc. Chambers of commerce, structured questionnaires, radio, television, the internet, etc. are the other information sources. Whatever the sources might be, the data must be reliable, accurate, complete, and up-to-date.

2. Persuasion:

To persuade means to make the other person determine to do something, particularly by constantly telling them or saying them the reasons why they must do it; in other words, trying to impact other individuals to believe or to do what one desires. This is one of the major aims of communication.

The vendor often significantly affects the buyer through persuasion to purchase his / her products, refusing to accept earlier decisions to purchase other products. This persuasion must be much planned that the purchaser becomes least aware of being convinced, and even if he/she becomes aware, he/she must be analyzed to think that it is for his / her own interest. Truly persuasion is an art that should be provocative in nature rather than exploitative.

3. Conveying suggestion:

Communication helps in expressing suggestions, opinions, and ideas. The workers who are directly connected in work know much better the flaws in it and can recommend to the managers the strategies to plug the gaps. This is an illustration of upward communication. In particularly large offices, recommendations boxes are given, and suggestions are obtained across the year. Sometimes further communication is made with the recommendations for clarity. Interaction of opinions and comments help the advancement of an organization.

Proposals are not in the nature of order or suggestions and are, therefore, never compulsory to follow them. Either rejection or acceptance is possible in the case of a suggestion. A suggestion may not be welcomed by certain executives, bosses, or managers who have a false notion of self-dignity, self-respect, higher role, etc., even though it is nice because it comes from lower levels. But in the interest of the organization, diverse executives accept positive feedback.

4. Advice:

Advising a person or a group of individuals is one of the aims of business communication. The director advises the subordinates on the ways and means to enhance efficiency. Advice needs personal judgment, and it affects the view and actions of the other person(s) to whom advice is given.

The business world of today is dynamic, and no one can be a master in all business spheres. So, on subjects on which he is not well-informed, a businessman has to take advice from experts. He may need advice on banking, insurance, stock exchange, tax laws, legal procedures, etc., for instance. The executives, supervisors, and managers may advise each other within the company (a horizontal communication case) and the subordinates (downward communication).

5. Motivation:

Communication is designed to motivate, inspire, and build a sense of commitment in the workforce. Their morale is improved by communication, and it leads to positive outcomes. Regular communication is essential to empower workers and implant in them a positive work attitude and a healthy relationship with managers. This, essentially, improves management efficiency.

Motivating someone implies encouraging someone but not pushing them to do something. An asset of every company is a motivated worker. The higher the motivation, the lower the cost of supervision since a motivated worker never ignores his obligations.

Monetary benefits, job security, job satisfaction, a healthy working climate, involvement in decision-making, targeting, etc. are motivating factors. As a strong motivator, money works. If extra salaries are permitted, a worker works overtime. Job protection motivates an employee to dedicate himself or herself to the job wholeheartedly.

If an employee is pleased with the work, he or she is happy to do so. In partnership with other stakeholders, a healthy working climate attracts him to work. The presence of staff in decision-making gives them a feeling of being part and parcel of the organization. Fixing an organization's production target, revenue target, etc. allows the staff to work together to accomplish the objective. Thus, multiple motivational variables contribute to an organization's success excellence.

6. Training:

In order to meet an organization's needs, senior staff may need to be trained to update them on new technological developments in order to adapt to changing work environments or job demands.

In order to cope with the methods, techniques, and working systems of the organization, new workers may also need training at the starting stage.

The key to all these types of training is communication. Through classroom teaching, seminars, lectures, short courses, conferences, educational tours, film shows, etc., communication can be achieved. In the above process, not only the ordinary staff, but the executive staff also need to be trained.

7. Instruction, direction, and recommendation:

One of the goals of business communication is to manage the staff by providing training, providing guidance, and arrangements for counseling. In a good business organization, legal, vocational, and medical advice and counseling are provided free of charge for the employees. The objective is to employ doctors, lawyers, coaches, etc. The underlying goal of such assistance is to keep the staff physically fit and mentally alert so that they can work for the organization's well-being wholeheartedly.

8. Giving warning and good job appreciation:

A good worker needs to be highly respected. It will motivate him to aim for improved results and greater participation. It makes the worker aware of his or her duties. On the other hand, workers who appear to be disciplined, non-accountable, and unproductive or cause chaos must also be warned. The purpose of both identification and alerts can be achieved through oral or written communication.

9. Utilizing resources:

Communication controls the misuse of corporate resources and helps to make efficient use of them.

The waste or misuse may be due to a lack of information or a lack of proper guidance in time.

Communication helps to bridge the information gap by training, feedback, etc. and minimizes waste or abuse of resources. Via contact, not only material resources but also financial resources, human resources, and other resources are properly utilized.

10. Management efficiency:

One of the aims of business communication is to improve management productivity. If there is a strong (formal and informal) contact network, the organization can be operated efficiently and effectively.

1.3 Importance of Business Communication

The importance or significance of business communication is rising day-by-day very quickly. Without the help of communication, the business world of today can't move smoothly. It makes a business enterprise complex and improves its effectiveness. It is considered to be the motivating force leading to industrial harmony.

For the attainment of organizational goals, it can be used as a device for controlling company activities. The role of communication in a company is as vital as the blood veins or arteries in the human body, according to Keith Davis. A business organization would cease to exist in its absence.

In management, business communication has an important role to play, the objective of which is to direct individual efforts in order to ensure the overall coordination of organizational activities. By transferring information, facts, and ideas and thereby making coordinated efforts possible, it performs the energizing function of the organization. As such, communication can be regarded as fundamental to the functioning of an organization.

Theo Haimann correctly said that, to a large extent, the success of management activities depends on a good communication system. Communication creates a favorable working environment, motivates employees to work hard, and thus facilitates management activities. It is possible to supply all the important and necessary messages or information at all levels of the organization through the communication process.

Business communication encourages managerial effectiveness and induces an organization's human elements to develop a spirit of co-operation that ultimately leads to peak performance. The leadership process is based on efficient communication. A key component of good labor-management relations is a sound communication system.

With the help of communication, the goals and policies that encourage co-ordination are better understood. In every company, the increasing importance of human relations with customers and employees has made communication the lifeline of the business. Producers are permitted to appeal to their customers about sales.

Subordinates are required to notify their superior of their grievances and complaints; otherwise, they may lead to conflicts. Proper communication helps to effectively implement decisions and leads to the company running smoothly. It creates mutual faith and credibility and builds the morale of employees and, therefore, provides them with job satisfaction.

In management, business communication is all the more valuable because the progress of an enterprise depends on how efficiently its staff understands each other. The majority of business issues can lead to poor communication between executives and employees.

So, poor communication or lack of communication will affect a business in different ways. It will have a major effect on employee understanding, put them in complete confusion, generate apathy for their work, hinder their willing co-operation, put co-ordination out of gear and encourage dislocation, chaos, and conflict in all business activities, and ultimately, the company's very survival will be at stake.

In recent years, the importance of effective communication in management has been widely acknowledged. It has become one of the most significant variables in management's efficient performance. It has an important bearing on management matters from different points of view.

The above discussion of the importance of business communication can be described as follows:

1. Informational movement:

Communication helps to move data from one location to another and from one individual to another. It creates an understanding chain among employees in a business enterprise at different levels.

2. Efficient and smooth running:

The effective and smooth functioning of an enterprise depends entirely on the efficacy of the communication system. It provides the basis of direction and moves individuals to act in accordance with the management authority's desires. Pursuant to G. "R. Terry:" communication serves as the lubricant that fosters the smooth management process operation.

3. Promoting management efficiency:

All the functions of business management are surrounded by communication. So, without it, no business management function can proceed toward its desired goal. It is an instrument of efficiency in management.

The efficiency of management relies on getting things done by other people by letting them understand and know what the manager wants them to do. It is the role of communication to keep the workers aware of everything that is required for smooth work results.

4. Appropriate planning:

Communication in the planning of business activities is very helpful. This provides the managers with the necessary information and ideas for sound planning. "According to Theo Haimann," Business policies and practices can be formulated and administered only through good communication. "Information secrecy creates and separates suspicion among employees. To show a better record of their performance, recognition of the common issues unites them.

5. Basis of decision-making:

Communication helps managers to make important decisions and to carry out vital activities. The quality of the decisions taken in an organization depends entirely on the quantity and quality of the data or information available to the management body. It may not be suitable for top management personnel to come into closer contact with their subordinates in the absence of efficient communication.

6. Foundation of co-operation:

Communication paves the way for co-operation by promoting mutual understanding and the meeting of minds. Before their actual performance, communication creates a condition for mental acceptance of the job. The will-to-do prior to actually doing it is this mental acceptance. Communication requires knowledge of and willing acceptance of orders and instructions and serves as the foundation for individual and cooperative efforts.

7. Ensures co-ordination:

Co-ordination requires orderly team attempts to ensure co-ordination of action. This harmony of action is the result of teamwork, which, in turn, depends to a great extent on a clear understanding of the organizational objectives, the way they are accomplished, and the work situation. The function of business communication is to inform employees fully of all work-related matters and to bring a perfectly tuned harmony to their work.

8. Satisfaction with Job:

Mutual trust and faith are extended by a proper communication system. It thus generates confidence in their manager's ability, promotes their loyalty to the company, and stimulates their interest in the job. The proper communication system allows subordinates to bring their points of view, grievances, and problems to the managers' notice. This facility tends to raise the morale of the employees and, ultimately, leads to high-performance job satisfaction.

9. Establishment of public relations:

An organization comes into contact with a variety of social classes, such as clients, investors, labor, unions, government, and local communities. In order to establish a favorable picture, it must maintain cordial ties with each of these classes. It must constantly strive to convince the general public that its actions are carried out in the interest of society. Without communication, no public partnership can be constructed.

10. Foundation of successful leadership:

Through communication, effective leadership is created. Through communication, the ideas, instructions, directions, etc. of the leader or manager are transmitted to the subordinate employees.

By wiping out confusion and mistrust between leaders and subordinates through communication, the manager may influence them and build a healthier relationship.

11. Motivation improvement:

Motivation is produced by communication. Through this, managers and staff are well-acquainted with the latest organizational knowledge. This leads to avoidance of hostility, recognition of the fact, change of mindset, understanding of accountability, and willingness to work ultimately.

12. Loyalties:

When they become aware of the competence of their boss's effectiveness through communication, the confidence and loyalty of the lower workers on the management staff increases, it helps to strengthen mutual trust.

13. The accomplishment of objectives:

Communication achieves organizational goals through collaboration and co-ordination between managers and employees. Through an effective communication system, interconnections between managers and subordinate employees are created.

14. Peace of industry:

Workers' unrest today is a concern. It communicates in the industry that can create peace. Two-way communication helps to build mutual understanding and co-operation. The management staff gives their orders, directives, guidance, etc. to the subordinates through downward contact.

On the other hand, upward contact enables the subordinates to express their requests, grievances, complaints, suggestions, etc. to their superiors. Thus, industrial peace can be created through the exchange of facts and knowledge between superiors and subordinates.

1.4 Steps to set up a Communication Process

For the happiness of your staff and clients, a solid business communication process is essential. This ultimately leads to financial stability. Twenty-nine percent of employees believe that their current internal communication tools do not work, one report found. Some of the reasons they listed are here:

Irrelevant information, dishonesty, exclusion, and lack of access to key information are likely to be experienced by your own workforce, too.

A Salesforce study found that 87 percent of executives, staff, and educators consider the reason behind workplace failures to be inefficient communication.

The importance of chemistry, understanding, teamwork, and their influence on employee productivity, engagement, and advocacy can no longer be ignored. Here are the tips to ensure a successful process of business communication that you can follow.

1) Audit your current state of communication with business and set goals

You need a communication plan in position, no matter the stage of your company. However, if you concentrate on the areas that need the greatest development right now and work your way to all other aspects, later on, you will make it the most useful.

For instance, these could be some of the reasons that your communication needs to be revisited:

- Low satisfaction with employees or high turnover
- Lower than expected performance across the organization
- Fast growth that leads to a loss of track of data

- Lack of transparency in information due to remote work

More than one of these, or a totally change scenario, you might experience. Identify it and set targets based on it for your business communication process. Your objectives, for instance, may include:

- A particular turnover or satisfaction rate of employees
- The satisfaction rate of customers
- Number of finished projects
- Number of departments' interactions and more

2) Identify core groups and their relationships with each other in your organization

Look into your organization's structure and all the groups involved in its ability to function. Take note of every group that needs data to function. This ought to include:

Departments (operations, design, marketing, human resources, sales, customer support, finance, and more) Horizontal classification, i.e.

Classification vertical: team professionals, team leaders, department managers, supervisors

External groups: clients, distributors, associates, and more

From here, they consider the work they do on an ongoing basis and the anticipated outcomes from them. In order for their work to get finished, plan out the way they need to connect.

This could be a major assignment, depending on your business size, so allow yourself plenty of time. Some of the main questions that require answering are:

What departments and individuals do they have to speak to on a regular basis? What about on a weekly, biweekly, and monthly basis? What kind of contact just happens when an external crisis occurs? How do administrators and team leaders in their teams achieve progress? How is reporting functioning? Is there a library of information that has the ability to decrease unwanted meetings and discussions?

What projects and procedures require the approval of other individuals in the company? How are requested and facilitated approvals?

These responses should at least give you an insight into the number of e-mails, texts, calls, meetings, and documents needed for anything to happen in the defined time frame.

3) Identify contact methods

Next, select the contact strategies that fit with your priorities for business communication, as well as the interactions in your organization between core groups. Review the list of communication methods that are mentioned earlier and make sure to add some special ones to your business:

- Communication-based on the internet
- Meetings by telephone
- Conference video
- Meetings face-to-face
- The records and official papers
- Introductions
- Boards for the forum and FAQs
- Surveys
- Activities in customer management

Which of these are important to achieving your goals for your organization? What's optional in adoption and may see resistance? Which ones raise the possibility of too many resources being added, and should they be simplified? About your individual needs, be practical.

A five-person start-up, where everybody works in the same office, would possibly concentrate on

- Communication-based on the Internet
- Meetings Face-to-face
- Control of customers

A 50-person, fully-remote organization will spend more capital in: Conferencing by phone and video to be able to faithfully monitor their operations, record organization. A large global company would certainly use many of the communication strategies mentioned and have dedicated teams for each of them.

4) Pick the right equipment

There is no handbook that determines for each reason which tools are completely best. Outlook vs. Gmail. Dropbox versus Google Drive. Slack vs. Chat with Nextiva. The wars go on, but the decision is entirely up to you and the workforce's preference. These tips are helpful:

To store significant documents and other materials, use cloud storage. To avoid human error and to forget to manually save information to it, allow automatic sync and backup.

- **Using a single e-mail and calendars platform.**

Utilize a single chat messaging tool. For instance, it will create friction and slow down communication if some people use Slack and other Hangouts in their Gmail.

If several of your meetings occur remotely, introduce an easy-to-use, secure business VoIP phone system.

Establish a brand and editorial guidelines outlining the voice tone and the use of elements of the brand. This way, all communication, internally and externally, is unified.

5) Record the process

Finally, throughout this setup, take note of everything you do and turn it into a shared document visible to the entire organization.

This way, each employee can refer to a communication plan that has been intentionally developed and choose the best action for the circumstance they are in. The document will also help newly on-boarded staff to understand all the tools and best communication practices easily.

For yourself and your team, you can develop a recurring calendar reminder to revisit the document once per quarter. This way, you will guarantee that the plan is still serving its best purpose and, if necessary, update it.

Your success in business begins with communication. For an organization, poor communication carries too many risks to count. Great interaction, though, provides an opportunity for excellent employee and customer engagement. This provides transparency, more significant outcomes, and sales and profit growth.

1.5 Impacts of Ineffective Communication

A company is doomed to fail without efficient communication. Not only does poor communication have an effect on your employees and company morale, but it can also affect your relationships with your customers.

Proper communication is required in the workplace so that your company can thrive, enabling you to meet customer demand, exceed business goals, and build strong relationships within and outside the company.

In fact, the biggest reason for employee unhappiness is poor communication. A 2014 survey found that because of communication problems, including lack of direction and constant change, 62 percent of staff don't like their jobs. Here are ways in which weak communication ruins your company and what you can do about it.

1. Unfulfilled expectations

The key to keeping your clients satisfied and happy is to always exceed expectations and come back for repeat business. You are likely to face unmet expectations when poor communication is common throughout your business, which in turn leads to unhappy and unsatisfied clients.

There's nothing worse than having missed customer meetings as a business owner or not meeting a deadline. This often happens when there is no one who communicates priorities and expectations clearly in a leadership position.

Make sure your staff is well informed of their everyday tasks and meetings to avoid upsetting customers. Use calendars with information about who is working on what and who needs to be where on what day, or a large whiteboard. Everyone understands which projects have priority in this way.

2. Highly stressful environment

The ideal atmosphere for stress is created by poor communication. Your staff will constantly be on the edge because nobody communicates due dates, assignments, and future projects. Your workers get the impression that everything is urgent without knowing which assignments are most important and what's going down the pipeline.

This leads everyone to feel anxious, rushed, and nervous. High stress leads to overworked workers, yourself included! In addition, you not only have to contend with bad communication, but you're also left to face low morale and reduced productivity of employees.

Schedule regular meetings that happen daily or weekly to avoid having a chaotic workplace. Speak about existing activities and future projects that workers need to be informed of during these sessions. Such meetings are often the perfect opportunity for workers to share any concerns or roadblocks they encounter.

3. Customer relations breakdown

Bad communication affects not only workers but also consumers. The secret to taking care of your clients is to communicate and collaborate with them regularly to ensure that their needs are addressed. Have you ever checked your inbox or listened to your voicemail, only seeing or hearing an angry client's message?

A bad impression of your company is generated by skipping a business meeting you arranged weeks earlier or failing to return a phone call. Because of this, relationships with your customers will begin to collapse, especially if poor communication is not immediately addressed.

Straying away from the kinds of content your customers want counts as well, so make sure you keep tabs on your website. Using lead generation plugins is critical because you can get details on your website about your client's time. Keep going for the content forms that people spend the most time on.

4. Impoverished customer support

When the workers do not have the data they need to do their job efficiently, they are less likely to do their job accurately.

Customer service and customer loyalty are impacted over time by poor communication and mismanagement. It will still influence the quality of service that customers get by not providing their workers with the data and support they need to do the job right.

Aside from productivity, poor communication often leads to confused and unhappy workers. Many clients pick up on these emotions when the workers feel unprepared.

The answer here is to get your workers ready. Make sure they get what they need to be successful so that they can better assist customers in turn. A study showed that happy staff contributed to an improvement in customer satisfaction of 1.3 percent. This then increased income and sales!

5. Uptick in absenteeism by workers

If the work/life balance and the overall morale of the workers are compromised by poor communication, they will continue to search for ways to escape the chaos that is work. Some are going to search for jobs outside the organization, while others are going to take more time off work just to escape.

Although everybody needs time away from work, it's a concern to know that workers are taking off because of the business climate. The risk of missing deadlines rises even further when an increasing number of workers turn up less frequently.

To prevent these conditions, aim to have flexible hours or remote job opportunities if you can. Even if an employee is not physically in the workplace, how can the problems of absenteeism be prevented by the opportunity to communicate to work? You can also use your site as a means of communication, and when they visit, your team and guests are sure to search safely with the best security plugins. Security makes workers and clients feel safe, and it's a nice feeling to be safe.

6. The high turnover

Bad communication is also likely to trigger high turnover rates alongside increased absenteeism. It is definitely helpful to have new faces and ideas coming into the business, but not when it comes to the expense of losing workers who have history and are embedded in the business.

Losing long-time staff can have a big impact on your company. New hires need to be educated, and you'll be left with a revolving team of new people as current employees continue to leave.

Poor communication is a common issue, but one that can bring the largest businesses down. It is best to fix poor communication until it begins to chip away at the success of the business to prevent dissatisfied employees and, therefore, dissatisfied customers.

Chapter 2: Types of Business Communication

In the business world of today, communication is a compulsion. People, including workers, owners, banks, clients, suppliers, advertisers, etc., either work for or are affiliated with an organization. Therefore, to achieve business goals as well as meet their requirements, they need to collaborate and interact with each other.

Let us take into account the various ways in which interactions take place in an organization. It is possible to define business communication by its structure, direction of information flow, modes of communication, and response.

Company correspondence styles: company communication styles vary depending on the following:

1. Structure-based

According to structure communication style is of two types:

- The formal
- Informal

2. Dependent on the medium

Depending on the medium communication style is of the following two types

- The Verbal
- Non-Verbally

3. Based on the direction of flow

Based on the flow of direction, communication styles is of the following four types:

- Upward
- Downward

- Horizontal
- Vertical

4. Response based

Based on response communication is of the following two types:

- The one-way
- The two-path

2.1 Structure-Based Communication Styles

The first is the communication structure; a crucial function is played by the channel used for interaction. The following two groups can be further bifurcated: On the basis of structure.

1. **Formal**

It is a daily and structured channel within an organization for work-related communication, where workers have to communicate among themselves through a proper medium.

Formal communication network types:

A communication network is a designed pattern to explain how data flows from one person to another. Now, let us go through the various networks created by structured communication:

Chain: A chain pattern is formed when an employee transfers official information to the other workers, who further communicates it to a third worker. For instance, the CEO informs the General Manager of the sales target, and the GM also transmits it to the Sales Manager.

Wheel: A wheel pattern is created when a single employee communicates some organizational data to a group of co-workers. For example, a circular released by the management in front of other co-workers was read by the team leader.

Circular: An employee gives his colleague details, who passes it on to another co-worker, and so on. The message goes from one worker to another and ultimately reaches the person who initiates the operation.

Free flow: No specific pattern is followed in this kind of network. Knowledge is transmitted by someone in a non-systematic manner. In an emergency situation in the company, for example, in the case of a short circuit, the information is distributed among the employees randomly.

Inverted: The subordinates may interact directly with their immediate senior, as well as their senior or top leadership, under this network. Sales executives, for instance, can meet with both their team leader and the manager.

2. Informal

It is an unofficial mode of communication resulting from friendship or informal relationships, in which the conversations may or may not be connected to the company or the job.

- **Types of informal communication networks:**

While no specific structure is followed for informal communication, the four informal networks are still defined as follows:

Single strand: Similar to the pattern of the chain, the knowledge goes on passing from one person to another in one strand, too; then to the next; and so on.

Gossip / Grapevine: Within an informal group, one single individual spreads information where the message may or may not be valid. This pattern is often termed as the grapevine.

Probability: It's similar to the pattern of gossip, but here, it's not necessary for everyone to engage in communication.

Cluster: When a person transmits knowledge only to his trustworthy people who feel that they are not going to tell others, but they are doing the same thing. The message thus spreads to a selected group of people; a cluster is known as this network.

2.2 Dependent on the Communication Medium

The way in which a message is designed and the channel used to transmit data to the recipient defines the following modes of communication:

1. **Verbal Communications**

The transmission of knowledge that is used in words is known as verbal communication, whether written or said. The word verbal means 'connected to words and word use.' Verbal communication is any communication using words. The most accurate and powerful symbol sets are words. Words signify meanings as well as to connote them. That is why, generally, all serious or formal communication is in words. Words may be written or spoken, as we are all conscious. Therefore, verbal contact can be divided further into two types:

a. Oral correspondence:

A speech-inflicted wound is more painful than a sword-inflicted wound.' Communication through the spoken word is, as the term itself implies, known as oral communication. Nine percent of the work time spent on verbal contact is written, 16 percent read, 30 percent speak, and 45 percent listening.

Words should be selected very carefully in oral speech so that what they connote has the same shade of significance.

Typically, the sender of the message or his representative is the speaker, while the listener is the recipient or his representative. A significant part of oral communication is listening, as well.

1. Factors in interacting orally:

Several factors are involved in oral communication:

- The speaker
- The manner in which he speaks
- What's he talking about?
- Who he is referring to
- Whether or not he gets feedback

2. Oral contact pre-requisites:

- Clear and proper word pronunciation
- Clarity and accuracy
- Conciseness
- Right tone
- Style and language

3. Merits of talking orally:

There are several advantages of oral communication:

- **Time and money savings:**

As well as time, oral contact saves money. No money has to be spent on the development of oral communication because only the spoken word is involved. Therefore, oral contact is economical.

Secondly, from the moment the sender sends the message, and the recipient receives it, there is hardly any delay. As soon as they are spoken, the words are heard and understood. Hence, oral contact saves time, too.

- **Instant feedback:**

The input is immediate in most oral communication. As soon as they are spoken, the words are heard, and the receiver can also instantly offer his reaction. The speaker will assess the mood and the listener's response. A benefit for the speaker is the immediate feedback.

- **Preserves documentation:**

As contact is in the form of spoken words, paperwork is minimal.

- **An effective instrument for exhortation**

You should try to reassure the audience when the conversation is verbal. Doubts can be quickly eliminated.

- **Constructs a balanced climate:**

When you talk verbally, a comfortable environment is created because there is less formality. On the basis of the input and response from the listener, you can also make changes to the communication immediately.

- **Best emergency tool:**

The fastest tool during an emergency is oral communication. When an immediate and quick response is critical, it is the best communication tool.

4. Oral contact demerits (limitations):

There are a few disadvantages of oral communication:

- **Greater chances of incomprehension:**

You will not refer to an oral message again unless it is registered. There are, therefore, higher risks of confusion or misinterpretation of a message. There is also an opportunity, in reality, that the message will not be understood at all.

- **Weak spokesperson:**

Better outcomes can only be obtained by a person who can fulfill all the requirements of successful oral communication. A bad speaker could send the wrong message more often than not. One communicates by articulation, voice modulation, and body language while speaking, too.

Where there is a disharmony between these elements, a message can be misunderstood. Also, what the terms connote and what they signify should be in harmony, as stated earlier; otherwise, the message can lead to a conflict of understanding.

- **Ineffective for prolonged communication:**

For lengthy correspondence, oral communication is not useful. There is every chance that anything important will be left out due to human weaknesses.

- **Lower rate of retention:**

Oral communication suffers from the downside of a low rate of retention. As the attention span varies from person to person, a listener can absorb only some portion of an oral message. People often seem to swiftly forget an oral note.

- **No statutory validity:**

Oral contact lacks documentary evidence. No permanent record or evidence of what has been said is available. It may be disputed later by an individual who has given a letter; similarly, an individual who has been given an oral letter or order may state that he has never received it. Hence, from a legal point of view, oral contact has very little meaning.

- **Liability is difficult to fix:**

Because a message is conveyed orally, transparency is difficult to address. In the execution of a message, this can often lead to carelessness.

b. Written communication:

When placed in black and white, a letter constitutes written communication. It is a structured type of communication. The writer constitutes the sender of the message or his representative.

In business organizations, written communication is usually considered binding and is often used as proof. The range of written communication by email and other such facilities has been expanded by technological development.

1. **Factors in written interaction:**

- The writer
- Content
- The vocabulary of the language used
- The object of the communications procedure
- The adopted style, formal or friendly
- Receiver

2. **Documented communication pre-requisites:**

- How much to publish
- What needs to be left out?
- When to leave
- When to communicate
- By what means is it transmitted?

3. **Merits**:

Correct and precise: Generally, written correspondence is prepared with great care and accuracy. The very prospect of writing makes an individual conscious. When communicating in written form, you have to be very serious and coordinated since written correspondence is subject to verification.

Checked easily: It can be read and re-read as written correspondence is on paper etc. It also makes itself available for verification. There is also, thus, less potential for others to distort the message to his or her own benefit.

Standing record: A permanent record constitutes written correspondence. It also behaves like evidence. For future reference, it is very beneficial, since it can be stored for years. Old orders and decisions, for instance, may serve as the base for new ones.

Ideal for lengthy and complicated communications: It is easier to comprehend long and complex messages when they are in written form rather than in oral form. There is less room for misinterpretation and confusion. The vocabulary used is, therefore, less susceptible to modification.

Liability can be set easily: The roles of the sender and recipient can be conveniently fixed in written correspondence. People prefer to transfer blame for errors, but if the burden is apparent in black and white, it is difficult.

Has constitutional validity: As a legal document, written correspondence is appropriate. Written correspondence, since time immemorial, has been used as proof.

4. **The demerits:**

1. Slower communication method:

Written communication can take time because it can take two or even three days (for example, by letters) to reach the recipient. Oral communication, by comparison, is immediate.

2. Additional delay if clarification is required:

Written interaction hampers quick explanations. For clarification, the receiver may write back and wait for a reply, making the process tedious.

Even if clarification is not required, there is still a delay between the time a message is written by the sender and received by the recipient.

3. Too much paperwork leads to:

Since written communication is essentially done on paper, paper-free offices remain a dream because one may tend to use it as an escape mechanism.

4. Always the possibility of ambiguity or the absence of understandability:

It is quite possible that the recipient cannot understand the precise meaning of a written message he has received. A written message's clarity also depends on the sender's ability or lack thereof. If the message has not been properly written, it will also not be understood.

5. Expensive in terms of money and hours for men:

Writing letters is not only an expensive task because you need to spend money on postage, but also because many people are involved in the process of sending a letter from an entity. Their time costs money for organizations. Although oral communication can be quick and efficient, written communication tends to be lengthy because of its very nature.

6. No versatility whatsoever:

After correspondence, the written word is not subject to immediate alteration. Conveying an afterthought, therefore, will prove to be quite long and, at times, even difficult.

7. Critical literacy:

It goes without saying that the person sending, as well as the recipient, should be literate in written correspondence. We can, in fact, wrongly assume that they are so. For large numbers of illiterate citizens, a written message would be irrelevant in many Asian countries where literacy is poor.

In the language of the post, literacy also implies literacy. The recipient should be familiar with the language in which a message was written. If you don't understand the language, getting a message in English is not useful.

Despite its shortcomings, it can be confidently inferred that the spine of an entity remains written correspondence. The written form includes almost all formal communication.

Aids for visuals:

A visual aid is a tabular, graphical, schematic, or pictorial illustration. Visual aids help communicators get their message out to their audience more efficiently. Visual aids help to make the content more engaging, explain and simplify difficult concepts, and highlight key points for the viewer to better retain them. Here are tips for generating powerful visuals:

- The visuals should be straightforward and easy to understand and should contribute to the overall comprehension of the subject through the design and layout.

- The graphics should correctly reflect the data, and important points should be stressed.

- For the target audience, the graphics should be acceptable.

- It is important to take note that the type-face and fonts are simple and readable and that the captions are brief and informative.

2. Communication Non-Verbal

When we hear 'actions speak louder than words,' it is known as non-verbal communication to convey data other than words. Without the use of non-verbal means, any contact stays incomplete.

Scientific research has shown that 55 percent of successful communication consists of body motions and gestures. Non-verbal contact, therefore, deserves considerable attention. Stuff such as movements, stance, physical appearance, etc. includes non-verbal communication. It takes place without words being written or spoken.

Those signals that are conveyed by means other than linguistic are non-verbal communication. While you may refuse to talk or write, it is difficult to prevent non-verbal actions. In two separate ways, non-verbal contact is defined here:

- Kinesics or body language: body movement, facial expressions, posture, etc.
- Auditory features-Paralanguage
- Proxemics-Space
- Environments
- Silence

1. Kinesics:

The study of stoat body activity is known as kinesics as part of non-verbal communication. It is an important part of our relationship. As a receiver, non-verbal contact should be detected 55 percent of the time. Our body delivers messages, moods, behaviors, etc. consciously as well as unconsciously, in the same way, that language uses collections of symbols to express meaning.

2. Facial phrases:

It is said that the face is the mirror of the mind. Whatever you think is mirrored on your forehead.

The face is able to express energy, frustration, sorrow, sincerity, and a host of other emotions and feelings.

A smile implies friendliness, while a frown implies anger.

Although a raised eyebrow shows surprise, a creased forehead shows concern, so it is very important to exercise discipline and control over our feelings. While this is a challenging challenge, with continuing efforts, you will get good results.

3. Gestures:

Gestures are small motions of the body that convey some message. It may also be the passing on of unique data. Some movements may be deliberate, whereas others may be accidental. Some movements, including a headshake for a "no" or a handshake as a "hello," have an almost universal sense.

Other gestures that may have regional meanings are then present. Strictly speaking, gestures are part of the language of the body because our heads and hands appear to communicate in their own way by themselves.

4. Posture:

The attitude assumed by the body is posture. This assists in conveying a message. There are expressive or protective roles in each action or location of the body. Thus, in non-verbal communication, posture is an essential factor. It exhibits a great deal about a person.

Posture involves the body's absolute bearing. The angle of inclination and the location of the arms and legs are included. A raised head suggests openness, while interest is suggested by a tilted head.

One should note, though, that none of these postures have any special meanings of their own. In conjunction with other symbols and in the sense of communication, they gain meanings.

5. Dresses:

By his appearance, a man is always judged. In improving his personality, his clothes play a significant role. A sad figure may be cut by shabbily dressed folks. For one to look professional and successful, it is important. In non-verbal communication, accessories often play a significant role.

Physical as well as socio-cultural features apply to clothes and accessories. Sometimes, accessories and clothes manage to live up to the receiver's standards, while sometimes, by violating these standards, they send a warning.

6. Eye contact:

The keys to the soul are the eyes. A very significant factor in face-to-face communication is eye contact. The speaker receives signals by eye- contact if the communication channel is available.

Discomfiture or nervousness only contributes to brief eye contact; on the other hand, curiosity is indicated by a long and fixed look. We have laughing eyes, angry eyes, painful eyes, evasive eyes, and so on, depending on our feelings

7. Quietness:

Louder than words, silence talks louder. It sets out the relationship and attitude between communicators towards each other. The inability to further converse is demonstrated by silence. When the teacher asks him for it, a student who has not completed his homework will remain silent.

- **The non-verbal communication indicators:**

1. **Positive ones**:

The positive indicators include:

- Smile
- Posture opened

- An expression that is interested
- Mild contact with the eye
- Correct speech pitch and volume

2. **Negative**:

The negative indicators include:

- Speech floundering
- Arms / legs defensive
- Sluggish debate
- Fretting of phrases
- Delusive looks

1. **Aggressive-:**

The aggressive indicators include:

- A tough voice
- Finger wagging
- Voice
- Supercilious phrases
- Immoderate contact with the eye

a. Language of the body:

Body language relates to the way the body communicates, by the movement of its pieces, without words. Our thoughts and feelings are conveyed by the nodding of our heads, blinking of our eyes, waving off our hands, shrugging off our shoulders, etc.

The signals that the body sends out to interact are all these gestures. That is why body language has been named this field of research.

Much as a language uses symbol sets to express meaning, our body conveys signals, emotions, moods, relationships with status, etc., both consciously and unconsciously.

Body language is very critical. It has been observed that we can play with words quickly and loosely, but our body speaks the facts. Our body, our eyes, our gestures, even if we try to hide the truth or whatever we want to suppress, can speak out loud and clear.

b. Paralanguage / language:

Paralanguage is the world of communication that includes signs, symbols, pitch, tone, and fluctuations for conveying meaning. Para stands for 'like' or 'akin.' Paralanguage means "like language," but not a language, in fact.

Anything in the proper way of the word that performs the role of communication as a language without becoming a language falls under the purview of Paralanguage. Paralanguage is used to define a wide variety of vocal features that help convey and represent the mood of the speaker. Since it does not consist of words, it is non-verbal.

The content of the message is concerned with verbal contact. What is being conveyed? Paralanguage, on the other hand, is concerned with the way in which the message is conveyed-how is it conveyed?

Speech, intonation, pitch, pause, volume, tension, movements, and signals are all based on Paralanguage. One's voice can express excitement, trust, anxiety, and the mental state and mood of the speaker through volume and pitch variation, stress on words, etc.

c. Voice:

The first signal we receive or use is the voice. A good listener can gauge a great deal from the pitch of the voice itself. Various types of voices are present.

A voice can, among other things, be sweet, gentle, musical, cultivated, friendly, nasty, clear, or indistinct. The voice will help expose the context, mental state, education, gender, and disposition of a speaker.

d. The intonation:

The change of the voice and the change in tension is intonation. Intonation is a part of interacting efficiently. A message with extreme material, for example, should not be conveyed in a high tone but in a sombre tone.

e. Pitch:

The vocal slant of the voice is pitch. It is quite necessary because it shows the frame of mind of the speaker. An unexpectedly high pitch may represent restlessness. Perhaps an unchanging pitch is repetitive or monotonous, decreasing the attention span of the listener.

The pitch can also help us comprehend the social status of the speaker. An individual uses a higher pitch than a subordinate in a position of authority. A change in the pitch typically results from the flaring of tempers.

f. Break:

A message is emphasized by a delay. A pause is what a comma is to prose, to speak. A delay can lead to miscommunication at the wrong location. The difference between trees' and fruit trees is, for instance, huge.

2.3 Based on Path Flow

The direction in which message or information flows within a formal set up in an organization defines the type of communication it is.

The following are the four primary forms of communication-according to their direction: On the basis of the flow of direction.

- Upward communication:
- Downward communication:
- Horizontal
- Vertical

1. Horizontal Communication

When information is exchanged among two people carrying a similar position in the company, it is named horizontal communication. For instance, a sales manager provides the sales revenue sheet to the finance manager. Horizontal communication is a key practice used to improve the sharing of information in start-ups and large enterprises.

It shows that communication in the workplace plays an important role in the success of a company, taking into account the number of time employees spends in meetings, giving presentations, or sending e-mails to colleagues. As your business grows, you will therefore need to adapt your communication practices accordingly.

Horizontal communication, also called lateral communication, is the practice of sharing data within the same level of an organization between staff, departments, and units.

Businesses aim to enhance cooperation and problem-solving when using this method by encouraging the flow of messages from people at the same level. Therefore, horizontal communication provides a sense of unity within a team that works towards the same goals when the company grows.

Here is an instance of how managers communicate horizontally:

In addition, this type of communication is efficient because it enables employees from various departments to work together to solve issues and enhance productivity in a synchronized work environment.

- **Advantages**

Due to the number of benefits, this method offers, improving horizontal communication is a trend in business today. With horizontal interaction, companies can:

- Coordinate operations
- Enhance the problem-solving process
- Reduce misunderstandings
- Encouraging teamwork
- Boost job satisfaction
- Empower the workers
- **Disadvantages**

However, before introducing it in your office, there are a few drawbacks of using horizontal communication that you should remember. This strategy is capable of:

- It would be hard to retain the regulation.
- Time-consuming to be
- Creating conflicts between employees
- Inducing a lack of discipline
- Other forms of contact in business

The fundamentals of efficient horizontal communication are the following:

Recognition: Horizontal contact must be understood by the top executive as a practical and useful way to exchange a message.

Emergency communication: In order to make this communication system successful, it is important to view it as a means of emergency communication in order to address a specific problem quickly.

Direct supervision: The staff should be persuaded to make this system manager more successful.

Discipline: To make discipline more effective, to be maintained strictly at any level. Otherwise, leadership will be abused.

Clear understandability: Care should be taken to make it successful so that managers can have a clear understanding that horizontal communication is a functional part of the overall process of communication.

Increase in interdepartmental communication: To make it efficient, the organizational structure should be developed in such a way that interdepartmental communication opportunities can be ensured.

Act as a lubricant: departments must be built to make them efficient so that they act as a lubricant in order to use horizontal communication effect.

2. Vertical Communication

When the senior of a specific department needs to share some information with the employee of the other department and vice-versa, for instance, a human resource manager warns a sales executive about too many leaves.

Vertical communication involves communication up to and down the chain of command of the company," according to Stoner and his associates.

Vertical contact is a source of information up and down the hierarchy of the enterprise, according to Bovee and his associates.

Vertical communication is the communication that moves up and down in the company, along formal lines of reporting, according to Ricky W. Griffin. Vertical communication, therefore, is communication where information or messages flow within the organizational structure's top level and the organizational structure's bottom level.

- **Advantages of communicating vertically**

No company runs a single day without engaging with the superior and the subordinate. It is essential for the business to interact without upper and lower-level employees. The following are some benefits of a vertical contact system:

Subordinate message transmission: The upper-level management transmits their ideas, grievances, and recommendations to the subordinates via the upward path of the vertical communication system.

Maintains good labor-management relationships: under his contract structure, there is a structured flow of knowledge such that a good relationship can be created among superiors and subordinates.

Maintains organizational discipline: In a vertical communication structure, there is a chain of command. So, among the staff, a sense of discipline can be developed.

Explaining policies and schedule: Upper-level management will submit the policies and procedures to the subordinates via the vertical communication system.

Effective decision making: In order to take decision making in the organization, superiors needed different information. Superiors gather information from subordinate types with the aid of vertical communications.

Help in decentralization: Comprehensive vertical coordination between departments can be assigned to duties and responsibilities.

Avoid by-passing: the superior and subordinates exchange messages directly under this communication scheme. There is also no probability of by-passing.

Maintains the command chain: with a vertical communication structure, the correct chain of commands is easily preserved.

Assigning jobs and reviewing performance: Vertical contact promotes the staff's work assignment and work assessment.

Increase productivity: Appropriate orders are sent to subordinates, and their roles and obligations are executed accordingly, helping to increase both superior and subordinate productivity.

- **Vertical communication drawbacks**

While having many vertical communication advantages, there are some drawbacks mentioned below:

Delay process: A delay process is a vertical communication drawback. It maintains a long chain of command for knowledge sharing in large organizations.

Disturbing discipline: If the position of director of the boss is seen by the subordinates' suspicious eyes in this conversation, the chain of command and discipline can be broken.

Performance decreases: In nature, the downward direction of vertical contact is dominant. There is, therefore, no chance for the staff to become successful.

Data loss or distortion: To sustain a long channel, details may be fabricated by the workers. Thus, its originality could be lost by its contact data.

Reduces relationships: The relationship between superior and subordinate may be diminished by this contact system due to inability and inefficiency.

Slowness system: The slowest communication process is vertical communication because it involves going across an organization's different levels. It can become ineffective for this reason.

Negligence of superiors: Superiors may fail to give their subordinates a message in this correspondence.

- **Vertical contact styles or variations**

Vertical communication strategies are used as knowledge flows from superiors to subordinates or from subordinates to superiors. Vertical communication is particularly categorized, in accordance with its existence, among the following two types: In any organization, there are two forms of business communication, which fall under vertical contact.

- Internal
- External

1. Internal

Internal interaction is all contact that has to do with internal matters and interaction between employers and workers in different ways. And it acts as an exemplary means to resolve all employee grievances, thus increasing aspects of goodwill, work satisfaction, efficiency, and protection. This also helps to raise turnover and income. You have, under internal correspondence,

1. **Communication upwards**

This illustrates the flow of information from lower down in the hierarchy to those in higher positions, thus preventing the organization from experiencing a vacuum in terms of not only the correct reception of data but also solutions to other problems that the business may face. Undoubtedly, contact is a two-sided sword, but knowledge must start at the bottom and pass upwards for it to function effectively. Exchanging ideas and knowledge, increased staff enthusiasm, job satisfaction, and the provision of feedback are the advantages of upward contact with the employees.

2. **Communication from downward**

The flow of data and guidance from the organization's top levels to its lowest levels, outlining the task and the policies, is generally referred to as downward contact. These may be in the form of detailed instructions or guidance for a full project to be completed. However, only after the upward contact has been effectively instituted must you start setting up the process. This flow of information can be used to transmit important issues and orders, to announce decisions, and to facilitate joint consultations, collaboration, and morale, to increase effectiveness and to receive input.

2. **Answer based**

Communication in an organization can be separated as per the need for feedback or response. Following are the types of business communication, based on the response:

1. One-way communication

In one-way communication, the sender transmits the information to the recipient without obtaining any feedback or response — for example, an advertisement for a particular product on television.

2. Communication is two-way

When the sender shares any data with the recipient, and the recipient responds to such information in return, it is known as two-way communication. For instance, the manager discusses with the team the issue of low productivity, and they offer reasons for it.

Chapter 3: Methods of Business Communication

In both large and small business environments, several contact strategies take place. Understanding the availability, advantages, and disadvantages of the different solutions will help businesspeople select the most likely communication methods to connect with audiences. Communication today can take place in a number of the ways-in person, through print records, broadcast messages, or, more and more, online

3.1 Telephone Meetings

Many businesses are ignoring how important the conventional phone is when connecting with consumers in a world where connectivity, software, social and cloud are rapidly becoming the preferred way to do business. The telephone provides more intimate contact, giving organizations the chance to incorporate two-way consumer communication in real-time.

Technology has turned into the most crucial part of our lives that, without our smartphones or getting information at the click of a button, we find it difficult to envisage existence. Everybody knows how significant it is for a company to connect with customers and how hard it will be to function without a reliable phone system.

- **Made it simpler to do business**

The internet is a very effective tool and helps companies promote consumers' brand recognition and sales messages. But it can be tough for people to work with technology and not be able to communicate with an individual directly. This can lead to annoyance with customers and a lack of personal contact.

It is important nowadays to have great customer service with online options for your customers to contact your company, but so is the provision of an effective telephone system.

With an effective telephone system in place, your customers will be able to directly contact your company and get responses to their questions much faster than if communications are done by email or online platforms.

- **Telephone advantages**

In order to fulfill your requirements, it is necessary to take time to thoroughly understand what your business needs and priorities are to help you select the right telecoms system. An effective business telephone system streamlines good organizational and consumer contact. A quicker contact than email is offered by the telephone, which is more intimate and convenient, and simple to use.

Use a powerful and cost-effective phone system; the Avaya IP Office solution will connect your employees and customers easily and reliably. When the company does, it expands, quickly serving more customers and new capabilities. Keeping ahead of the competition means delivering a greater customer experience. Getting the right instruments in place will give the company that extra edge.

3.2 Video Conferencing

It is a technology that enables users to hold face-to-face meetings in distinct locations without having to move together to a single location.

For business users in various cities or even different countries, this technology is particularly convenient because it saves time, expenses, and business travel problems.

Video conferencing applications include holding routine meetings, negotiating company deals, and interviewing job applicants.

- **How video conferencing operates**

The main advantage of video conferencing over teleconferencing is that users can see each other, which enables them to establish stronger relationships. For informal purposes, when a video conference is held, it is called a video call or video chat.

There are numerous ways in which video conferencing can be carried out. Web cameras connected to built-in laptops, tablets, or desktop computers may be used by individuals. Smartphones that are equipped with cameras can also be used for video conferencing connections. Typically, a software-based platform is used to transmit communication over Internet protocols in such cases.

To ensure the interaction is clear and with limited technical faults, some companies use dedicated video conference rooms that have been equipped with high-grade cameras and screens. The hardware needed to conduct the video conference is often installed and assembled by third-party providers. With the speed and reliability of the data connection, the stability and quality of the video conference may fluctuate.

- **Video conferencing uses**

In order to encourage their teams to function more collaboratively, companies with multiple offices may create direct video connections between their locations.

It is also possible to use video conferencing as a tool for instruction, with the teacher teaching a remote class from almost anywhere.

This can be achieved in a corporate context, especially in order to provide employees with the information they require to do their work better. Video conferencing may also be used by the academic community to associate a typical classroom environment with students who have located a substantial distance from campus.

A video conference can also be used to hold daily meetings with employees of an organization or to speak to shareholders about the current business activities. It can be used to announce major changes in a company, such as the arrival of a new CEO or the interactive presentation of information that enables all participants to discuss what they see on the screen.

Video conferencing facilities are often made available by hotels and conference centers to visitors who need such facilities. This may be provided in suites or meeting rooms furnished for this reason.

- **Video conferencing benefits and drawbacks**

Video conferencing is the visual communication system in which live; face-to-face communication takes place without any transportation being needed. Video conferencing eliminates distance barriers and helps connect with the aid of the internet in real-time. It is commonly used by businesses to connect throughout the country and internationally with their workers and customers. It significantly reduces a company's travel costs, as it enables meetings, seminars, and training sessions to be held without requiring distant employees and customers to travel to the main location. Because each technology has both positive and negative aspects, video conferencing also has its own share of benefits and drawbacks.

- **Advantages**

Cost-cutting: Video conferencing helps to reduce a company's travel expenses.

It helps the company to communicate without any hassle with its employees and customers and share screens, images, HD audio, and videos.

Improves productivity: Video conferencing prevents work from being logged back, as it helps workers to address the concerns with the individual concerned without any delay. Simple communication availability eliminates communication gaps, thus reducing the probability of job pitfalls.

No time barrier: Video conferencing eliminates the time and place barriers by allowing a group of individuals to address items without shifting from their position with others who work in distant locations. This enables a smooth workflow without any breaks and hitches in the business.

- **Inconveniences**

Besides a lot of benefits, video conferencing have some drawbacks:

Technical problems: The malfunction of any part of the hardware or software can impede the smooth functioning of the job. Professional technical people are needed to rectify the issue. This will delay work and add to the company's maintenance costs.

Leads to misjudgments: A video conference meeting or interview may often lead to incorrect decisions and choices, as it becomes difficult to access a person's gestures and personality through this interactive medium at times.

Financial strain: It can be a financial burden for a small-scale organization to build a video conference system, as it is a bit costly technology and needs frequent maintenance.

HD Hitech is a pioneer in the installation at affordable rates of integrated video conferencing systems in commercial spaces, thereby improving their competitiveness and performance multiples.

3.3 The Memos

There are several styles of tools, each tailored to particular circumstances, for official communication. A memo is one such popular form of communication. Let us find out about their format and meaning and see examples as well.

- **What is a memo?**

In reality, a memo is short for a memorandum. In the business world, it is one of the most used forms of official contact. Its primary aim is to act as a reminder or to provide some direction. Again, these such circulars are a form of mass communication, i.e., to connect with a large number of organizational individuals.

We normally write a memo for one of the five reasons below.

- As a memento,
- Highlight an incident or condition
- To recount an occurrence.
- Keep an official record of whatever
- Passing data or instructions to

For over a century now, memos have been a common way to commute. This is because, as seen below, they have many advantages:

- They are a means of mass communication that is very cost-effective. And its transmission is very cheap, too.
- Its simplicity is another benefit. They are really easy to compose and comprehend.
- Memos tend to be short-lived and to the point. They even meet a number of individuals. So they are also really time-saving, too.

- They also act as proof in the event of a conflict.
- **The memo format**

Let us see the steps involved in writing a memo.

Heading: We type the word 'Memo' or 'Memorandum' at the top of the page in the center after the company's name and address (which is on the letterhead).

Recipient: To answer recipients in the correct way, example- 'To all sales division employees'

Writer: Write the name of the person who wrote the memo, such as 'From Mr. ABC, Head of Sales'

Additional recipients: These are the persons who will receive a copy of the memo for courtesy. The memos are not addressed to them, but we're keeping them in the loop.

Date: An important information that one must provide is the date of writing the memos.

Subject line: This will offer a quick idea of the details in the memos to the reader. The line has to be short, accurate, and to the point. Example- Subject: Meeting of all sales division employees.

The memo body: This is where it contains all the material. In a memo, a formal salutation is not needed. Just relay with clarity and precision the required details. Not too long must be the body. The ending must reaffirm the problem and finish on a positive note.

Proofread: Finally, prior to submitting it, proofread the memo.

3.4 The Letter

Letters are short messages sent to beneficiaries who are often outside the business.

They are often written on letterhead paper and are usually limited to one or two pages, representing the corporation or organization. Although today it is possible to use email and text messages more regularly, the business letter remains a popular type of written communication. It can be used to introduce you to a prospective employer, to announce a product or service, or even to express thoughts and feelings (for example, compliant letters).

In terms of type and content, there are many kinds of letters and many variations, yet the fifteen elements of a typical letter in block format. Letters can serve to introduce prospective employers to your skills and qualifications (cover letter), provide relevant or detailed information, provide event or decision documentation, or present an attached report or long document (letter of transmission). There are seven primary sections to a standard letter:

Letterhead/logo: Name and return address of the sender

Heading: the recipient's name, sometimes including address and date,

Salutation: "Dear" If known, use the name of the recipient

Introduction: sets out the overall intent of the letter

The body: articulates the message information.

The conclusion: the key point is repeated and could include a call to action

Signature line: It also includes the details of the contact.

Bear in mind that you and your business are reflected in your absence by letters. Note that, in order to connect effectively and project a positive picture,

- It should be simple, succinct, precise, and respectful of your language.
- Every word should contribute to your goal.

- Each paragraph should concentrate on one definition,

- A full message should be created by the sections of the letter.

- There should be no mistakes in the message.

Unique reasons letters

In a professional context, there are several potential explanations for why you would write a message. Here is a list of letter types that are the most common:

Transmittal letters: when you send to an external audience a report or some other document, such as a summary, send it with a cover letter that briefly describes the intent of the accompanying document and a short summary.

Letters of inquiry: You might want to request information about a corporation or company, such as whether they are expecting job opportunities in the immediate future or whether they are supporting grant proposals from non-profit organizations. In this situation, you will send a letter of inquiry asking for more information. Keep your request short, as with most business letters, addressing yourself in the opening paragraph and then explicitly outlining your intent and/or request in the second paragraph. Consider putting your requests in the list form for clarification if you need very detailed details. Conclude in a polite manner that reflects respect for the assistance you may receive.

Follow-up letters: Write a follow-up letter expressing your gratitude for the time your letter recipient has taken to respond to your needs or accept your work application if you have made a request from others. The follow-up letter thanking the interviewer for her or his time is particularly relevant for showing your attention and integrity to detail if you have had a work interview.

Letters can take on many other purposes within the professional context, such as interacting with suppliers, contractors, partner organizations, consumers, government agencies, and so on.

3.5 Email

To most students and staff, email is familiar. In industry, it has increasingly replaced external (outside the company) correspondence with typed hard copy documents and has, in many cases, taken the place of internal (within the company) contact memos.

For messages that have slightly more substance than a text message, email can be very helpful, although it is also best used for fairly short messages. To accept communications from the public or to inform associates that periodic reports or payments are due, many organizations use automatic emails. You may also be assigned to "populate" an email form in which standard paragraphs are used, but to make the wording acceptable for a specific transaction, you select from a menu of sentences.

In private settings, emails can be casual, but business correspondence involves attention to detail, the knowledge that your email represents you and your business, and a professional tone so that it can be forwarded if necessary to any third party. In organizations, email also serves to share data. Although email can have an informal feel, note that it needs to express professionalism and respect when used for company. Never write or submit something you wouldn't want to read in public or in front of the president of your organization.

Professional communication involves attention to the particular meaning of writing, as with all writing, and it might surprise you that even elements of the form may show the deep comprehension of the audience and intent of a writer. The concepts explained here also refer to the sense of education; use them when engaging with your teachers and peers in the classroom.

- **Efficient company emails guidelines**

Open with a proper greeting: in the event of a message being mistakenly sent to the wrong recipient, proper greetings display appreciation and prevent mix-ups. Using a greeting, for example, such as 'Dear Ms. X' (external) or 'Hello Barry' (internal).

Subject line: Include a simple, brief, and particular subject line. This allows the receiver to understand the message's essence. For instance, "Proposal attached" or "Project Y electrical specs."

Close with a signature: by generating a signature block automatically containing your name and business contact information, mark yourself.

Stop abbreviations: an email is not a text message, and ROTFLOL (rolling on the floor laughing out loud) will not be induced by your wit.

Be brief: omit words that are needless.

Use a decent format: For ease of reading, break your message into brief paragraphs. In three small paragraphs or less, a strong email should get to the point and conclude.

Reread, edit, and reedit: before you press "submit," catch and fix spelling and grammar errors. It would take more time and effort to undo the issues created by a hasty, badly written mail than to take out the time to get it accurate the first time.

Respond promptly: watch out for an emotional response, never respond in anger, but make a habit of replying within twenty-four hours to all emails, even if only to say that in forty-eight or seventy-two hours, you will provide the requested information.

Use reply-all sparingly: do not give your reply to anyone who got the initial email unless the whole community needs to read your response fully.

Stop using all caps: on the internet, capital letters are used to express emphatic feelings or shouting and are considered to be rude.

Test links: If a link is used, test it to ensure that it works.

Advance email: If you are going to attach large files, email in advance, audio and visual files are always very big; be careful to avoid hitting the mailbox cap of the recipient or activating the spam filter.

Send feedback or follow up: email or call if you don't get a response within twenty-four hours. The spam filter may have intercepted your letter, so it might never have been accepted by your recipient.

Tip: add the last recipient's address to prevent being sent prematurely. This will allow you time to do a final analysis of what you've written, make sure that links work, make sure that the attachment has been inserted, etc., before adding the address of the sender and hitting send.

3.6 The Texting

Whatever digital device you use, written correspondence has become a popular way to communicate in the form of brief messaging or texting. It is helpful for brief exchanges and is a convenient way to remain linked with others when it would be cumbersome to communicate on the phone. For long or complex texts, texting is not beneficial, and the viewer should be given due consideration.

Always consider your audience and your business while messaging, and use words, phrases, or abbreviations that will convey your message properly and efficiently.

- **Guidelines for efficient texting for business**

Keep the following points in mind if your job situation enables or requires you to communicate through text messages: Know the recipient:'? Percent dsct "may be a comprehensible way to ask a close associate what the best discount is to give a certain client, but if you write a text to your manager, it may be better to write," What percent discount does Murray get on a $1 K order?

Anticipate unintended misinterpretation: to reflect feelings, ideas, emotions, and texting also uses symbols and codes.

Be mindful of its limitations and avoid misinterpretation with brief texts, considering the difficulty of communication and the useful yet restricted texting method.

Use appropriately: it can verge on intimidation to contact anyone too often.

Texting is an instrument. If necessary, use it; just don't misuse it. Do not text and drive: evidence shows that if the driver texts behind the wheel, the risk of an accident increases dramatically.

Being in an accident while performing company business will reflect badly on your judgment as well as on your employer.

1. Netiquette

In a professional context, text messaging, emailing, and posting on social media requires you to be familiar with "netiquette," or proper etiquette for internet use. We have all heard news stories about people who have been fired and businesses boycotted for making offensive or inappropriate posts on social media. People have even gone to jail for using private messaging illegally. The digital world may seem like a "wild west" free-for-all, with no clear rules or regulations, but this is clearly a dangerous perspective for a professional to take, as it can be very expensive to break tacit rules, expectations, and guidelines for professional communications.

In writing, the way you represent yourself carries significant weight. It takes tact, skill, and awareness to write in an online environment that what you have written may be there for a very long time and maybe seen by individuals you never assumed as your intended audience. From text messages to letters to memos, from business proposals to press releases, you and your company are represented by your written business communication: your objective is to make it clear, concise, constructive, and professional.

As a normal part of our careers, we create personal pages, post messages, and interact via online technologies, but how we conduct ourselves can leave a lasting image, literally. Your potential employer may have seen the photograph you posted on your Instagram page or Twitter feed, or that insensitive remark in a Facebook post may come back to haunt you later.

As detailed below, following several guidelines for online postings can help you avoid embarrassment later:

- Know your background
- Present yourself

- Don't make assumptions about your readers; remember that culture affects the style and practice of communication.

- Get familiar with your organization's policies on the acceptable use of IT resources.

- Remember the man: Remember that behind the words, there is a person; asks for clarification before making a decision.

- Before you post, check your tone; avoid jokes, sarcasm, and irony, as they can sometimes be misunderstood and get lost in translation in the online world.

- Respond to individuals using their names

- Note that history, age, and gender can play a role in how individuals interact.

- Stay legitimate and assume the same of others.

Note that individuals will not immediately respond. Individuals engage in various ways, some simply by reading the conversation rather than leaping into it.

Recognize the permanent text

- Be judicious and diplomatic; it can be difficult or even impossible to withdraw what you say online later.

- Find your duty to the team and to the working environment.

- Agree on basic rules for text communication if you work collaboratively (formal or informal; seek clarification whenever necessary)

- Stop flames: study before answering.

- Allow and forgive errors.

- Find your duty to the team and to the working environment.

- Before responding, seek clarification; what you heard isn't necessarily what was stated.
- Ask for advice from your supervisor. *
- Value secrecy and original concepts

If you answer with a particular point made by someone else, quote the original author.

Prior to forwarding the communication, ask the sender of an email for permission.

Online behavior can often appear so disrespectful and even aggressive that attention and follow-up are required. In this scenario, let your boss know right away so that it is possible to call on the right resources to help.

2. Storing cloud

Cloud storage is a way of saving data securely online for businesses and customers so that it can be accessed from any place at any time and easily shared with that granted permission. In order to facilitate recovery off-site, cloud storage also offers a way to back up data.

People now have access to several free cloud computing services, including Google Drive, Dropbox, and Box, all of which come with upgraded subscription packages that offer larger storage sizes and additional cloud services.

- **Explained cloud storage**

Cloud storage provides a simple way too securely and safely store and/or move data. It allows individuals and businesses to keep their files on any of their devices stored with the cloud services provider for on-demand access. It is also possible to use cloud storage to archive data that requires long-term storage but does not need to be accessed often, such as certain financial records. "Files stored" in the cloud "are increasingly used for community collaboration.

Cloud storage works by allowing files to be sent and retrieved remotely by a client device, tablet, or smartphone to and from a remote data server. Usually, the same data is stored simultaneously on more than one server so that clients can always access their data even if one server is down or loses data. For example, in the event the laptop is stolen, a laptop computer owner could store personal photos both on her hard drive and in the cloud.

A cloud storage system may specialize in storing a specific type of data, such as digital photos or music files, or any type of data, such as photos, audio files, text documents, presentations, and spreadsheets, may be stored in general.

It is believed that cloud storage was invented in the 1960s by computer scientist Dr. Joseph Carl Robnett Licklider. Around two decades later, in order to store some of their files, CompuServe started to sell its customers limited quantities of disc space. AT&T launched the first all-web-based storage service for personal and company communication in the mid-1990s. A number of different services have gained traction since then. Apple (iCloud), Amazon (Amazon Web Services), Dropbox, and Google are among the most popular providers of cloud storage.

- **How businesses benefit from cloud storage**

By eliminating the need for data storage infrastructure on business premises, cloud storage helps companies with major data storage needs to save a significant amount of space and money. All necessary hardware and software are owned and maintained by the cloud storage provider so that the cloud users do not have to.

It may cost more in the future to buy ongoing cloud storage, but it can be significantly less costly upfront.

In addition, as their storage needs change, companies can almost instantly scale up or down the amount of cloud storage they have access to.

The cloud also allows employees to collaborate with colleagues and work remotely and outside regular business hours while allowing authorized employee's easy access to the most updated version of a file to facilitate smooth document collaboration. Cloud storage enables mobile data at a personal level and enables digital life in the holistic way we are living it today. Smartphones would not be able to interface with so much data (photos, documents, information on the go) without the cloud. The use of the cloud to store files may also have a beneficial impact on the environment because it decreases energy consumption.

Protection for cloud storage

In the digital era, there is so much focus on cloud storage today because so much of our confidential personal data is stored in the cloud, whether we store it there willingly or because a company in which we do business chooses to store it there. Cloud security has become a big concern as a result. Users wonder if their data is safe, and growing data breaches have shown that it often isn't. Users are also worried about whether, when they need it, the data they have stored on the cloud will be available.

While cloud storage may appear vulnerable because of the prevalence of hacking, security vulnerabilities are also present in alternatives, such as on-site storage. Company-provided cloud storage will potentially boost security by providing workers an opportunity to back up and move data that they need to access outside the office using their personal accounts.

There would be data replication with a successful cloud storage service, storing the same files in various physical locations so that any human mistakes, equipment failures, or natural disasters will survive. A reputable provider will also safely store and transfer data so that no one without authorization can access it. Some users will also request data to be stored in such a way that it can only be read but not altered; cloud storage also offers this feature.

3.7 Face-to-Face Meetings

New methods of communication, such as texting, email, and video conferencing, are quickly improving business communication face-to-face. According to a 2010 "University of Media" recent study by Mindshare business planning group, Alloy Media and Brainjuicer, only 29 percent of college students prefer face-to-face communication. Instead, more than 50 text messages are sent per day by students. They'll be more comfortable with new technology than previous generations as these young adults move into the workplace. Yet, in business, face-to-face communication plays a dominant role.

- **Advantages**

According to a Forbes Insights survey of more than 751 business professionals, the large majority of executives' still feel face-to-face communication is important for the business. In fact, eight out of ten respondents said they preferred face-to-face meetings over meetings such as video conferencing that are technology-enabled.

They said that face-to-face meetings "build stronger, more meaningful business relationships" while enabling better social opportunities to connect with customers and colleagues.

The reading of facial expressions, body language, and the interpretation of nonverbal communication signals are also easier. Face-to-face communication, overwhelmingly agreed by respondents, is best for persuasion, leadership, engagement, inspiration, decision-making, accountability, candor, focus, and consensus.

- **Restrictions**

Although face-to-face communication is usually preferable, remote communication benefits exist, writes Chuck Martin in the Chief Information Officer magazine. In cases where members can not interrupt their work schedules to meet, email, and instant messenger communication may speed up the discussion for large groups. Email is also a better way to plan and confirm meetings because, if necessary, everyone will have reliable, written correspondence to refer back to. A phone call is a more rational way to have a fast two-way conversation without time being blocked out. For longer context pieces that require an increased level of understanding and comprehension, memos are best. To quickly disperse corporate messages to staff, some company owners use DVDs, which is a short, entertaining way to catch attention.

- **Features**

'A little planning will go a long way,' writes Marty Nemko of Kiplinger. The most productive communicators do not know anything, but to focus on a significant niche where they are the experts, they have fine-tuned their speeches. At a face-to-face meeting where you can't google your way out, going into an encounter prepared is extremely important. Bring jotted notes, but a strict script is not read. Be frank, share a personal story, and draw out the empathy of your listeners to enhance trustworthiness.

Dig for content that is new and appropriate. In an engaging way, actively involve your listeners by asking questions or introducing activities to your meeting. "Finally, Nemko remembers," When you talk, think like a concert pianist: vary your sound, rhythm, and strength in virtually every sentence. Include dramatic pauses

- **Misconceptions**

Nectarios Lazaris, CIO of the global architectural firm Woods Bagot, told Forbes Magazine, "The only thing that gets lost (in video conferencing) is that people are not sitting in the same room. Other than that, it's the same." However, in a July 2010 issue of UX Matters magazine, Corrie Kwan, Jin Li, and May Wong write that remote usability results are just as good as face-to-face results. Facilitators cannot identify nonverbal signs without a way to observe research participants during remote usability trials, "the authors conclude, referring to the enduring value of face-to-face company contact." They maintain that many business interactions rely on nonverbal signals prompted by empathy, connection, and comprehension, which is hard to construct without meeting participants gathered in the same room.

- **Considerations**

In industry, time is the greatest impediment to face-to-face contact. Overworked executives frequently find like they simply do not have the time to meet and communicate in a constructive way with all employees. For instance, to optimize the time, meet with a handful of senior executives for a one-hour meeting on Monday to discuss the most critical problems of the week and request reports from different departments. Meet each individual member the next day to review updates and relevant messages that they have collected for you.

Meet with organizational executives on Wednesday and meet with front-line managers on Thursday.

Your front-line workers will have a new sense of direction by Friday. While you will meet with others face to face, for other staff to review, you can publish your meeting notes electronically online, thus keeping multiple communication channels open.

Chapter 4: Barriers in Effective Business Communication

There are many possibilities for why interpersonal communications can collapse. In many conversations, the message (what is said) might not be interpreted exactly the way the person wants. It is, therefore, critical that the communicator needs feedback to ensure that the message is properly understood.

The skills of Active Listening, Clarity, and Reflection can help, but professional communicator also needs to be aware of the obstacles to successful communication and how to avoid or resolve them.

There are several obstacles to communication, and these can arise at any point in the communication process. Barriers can lead to your message being distorted, and you also risk wasting both time and/or money by causing confusion and misunderstanding.

4.1 Barriers in Communication Process

All you need to think about the various barriers of communication: there are many obstacles to communication that tend to distort the messages that pass among the sender and recipient. It leads to confusion and conflict among the organizational members.

Managers frequently state that communication breakdown is one of their most significant problems. Communication issues, however, are often symptoms of more deeply rooted issues. For instance, the cause of uncertainty about the company's direction may be poor planning.

Similarly, a poorly designed organizational structure may not clearly communicate organizational relationships. Vague performance levels may leave managers uncertain about what is expected of them. Following are some common barriers:

- Semantic barriers
- Psychological barriers
- Organizational barriers
- Personal barriers
- Mechanical barriers
- Status barriers
- Perceptual Obstacles
- Information filtering
- Specialization,
- Time's reassurance
- Unclarified, hypothesis
- Inattentiveness.

1. Semantic Barriers:

This denotes barriers and their interpretation of language and symbols. Every language consists of symbols that are used to convey meaning from one individual to another. For communication purposes, even code and mathematical symbols are used in a language. The obstacles are due to the linguistic ability of the person involved in the interaction.

The various types of semantic barriers include the following:

a. Poor message quality:

It must be consistent in all respects when a message is prepared, such as clarification, consistency, and use of suitable terms to transfer the 'idea' to be conveyed. It should be easy, easily understood by the receiver in simple terms. Otherwise, it becomes non-specific, and the recipient will have trouble properly following it.

b. Defective transmission:

When the message is received from the superior to the subordinate, the person receiving it must be able to translate it into various categories of subordinates with the comprehension level constraints and their IQ. To help disseminate the information to the staff, it does require proper interpretation of the message received.

c. Inadequate clarity:

There are certain ideas in all the messages that need to be understood correctly. In other words, the meaning must be well perceived by the receiver between the lines of the message. If it isn't, the message is likely to be misunderstood, leading to confusion.

d. Technical vocabulary:

It is often seen that professional individuals use technical language in their communication. The average man does not know this. As far as possible, it must be in plain language, familiar to everyone, when interacting with ordinary people. Consider the example of a doctor, for instance, who prescribes medication to a patient and writes 'TDS' (three times a day abbreviation). If it is written in a clear language, or the abbreviation is explained to him, an average patient will not be able to understand this.

2. Psychological obstacles:

The psychological, mental state of the sender, as well as that of the person receiving the message, makes a great difference in interpersonal communication. His tone overpowers the script of the message when a person is emotional. In normal communication, this creates an obstacle that leads to emotional barriers. Psychological barriers are as follow:

a. Premature assessment:

The potential consequence of the message before it is sent to the recipient is this premature assessment. Such an assessment will prematurely assume that the message may not produce the desired outcome, thereby withholding the message. This is a significant psychological part of the barrier to contact

b. Insufficient attention:

Usually, this happens at the end of the receiver in communication due to carelessness and not listening properly to what the individual says at the other end. In fact, this takes place to face contact or to attend telephones.

b. Losses in transmission and low retention:

If a contact in an organization passes through multiple hands and stages, the transmission of the message by different individuals appears to become unreliable or corrupt. In writing, as well as verbal communication, this occurs. In the latter, because of poor retrieval capability, the recipient could not remember the message as it was transmitted to him, thereby contributing to a misunderstanding at a later stage.

c. Undue written message stress:

Every executive believes in a company that written notes, directions, and orders will be safer, as the chances of any miscarriage of the message are almost zero. When a message is exchanged face-to-face between a superior and a subordinate, it not only enhances comprehension but is also effective. It instills confidence in the subordinate as far as the execution of the instructions for orders is concerned. It is, no doubt, a better contact tool than the written one.

d. Lack of confidence by the recipient in the sender:

If the original correspondence is regularly altered by a communicator (sender), the recipient at the other end will usually postpone the action warranted by the message. Due to unpredictable decisions frequently made by the sender, this occurs. Thus, with different changes and additions, contact becomes inefficient. This is an instance of a lack of trust on the part of the sender.

e. Failure of communication:

The superior / manager often fails to convey the necessary information/order, etc. This may be the cause of the sender's flippant attitude or his apathy. For example, misunderstanding and embarrassment are likely to be caused by the sender's overconfidence that the message has already been communicated to people

3. Organizational obstacles:

This depends on the general organizational policy regulating the organization's contact network. Such a policy may be a written text that describes different aspects of communication, in particular, upward, downward, and lateral, as an efficient communication flow in the company is desirable. This part of the barrier is discussed below:

1. Restrictions imposed by organizational rules:

Usually, the data must be transmitted via the correct channel to higher-ups. When going down the hierarchical ladder, this gets postponed. It is important to provide instructions in general for passing messages. In order to prevent delays, detailed instructions for managing critical messages must also be clarified to everyone.

2. Status / hierarchical roles restrict the information flow:

In personal dealings, a person's standing and/or position make a lot of difference. In a formal organization, superior/subordinate capacity also prevents the free flow of communication. This occurs especially in the case of upward contact. An individual from the lower rung in the hierarchy may find it difficult to directly approach the organization's top executive.

3. The organization's complex situation:

Large companies, where there are a variety of layers of contact in management roles, can be skewed. When conveyed in the upward direction, this takes place because of the censoring of the message; since people are generally reluctant to tell the superiors of the adverse aspects.

4. Personal Obstacles:

These obstacles are those that exist in contact at different levels of the organization due to personal constraints, such as:

a. Superiors' attitude:

The superior's attitude plays a crucial role in the communication process, whether upward or downward or in some other direction. The superior's attitude, either favorable or unfavorable, thus determines the flow of contact, i.e., from superior to subordinate and vice versa.

b. Following the correct channel insistence:

Superiors advise their subordinates, when talking, to follow the right channel. They do not want a subordinate to circumvent them and go to the next higher authority directly. In order to allow them to know what is happening in their jurisdiction, they still want to be in contact with the communication process.

There may be a need to circumvent the superior during an emergency situation; the superior may not, however, like it. He may prevent it and instruct the subordinates to keep it in the picture as and when occasions arise with whatever information/message is passed to higher up.

c. Lack of subordinate trust:

It is a common assumption that, because they do not have the capacity to do so, subordinates are not qualified enough to advice superiors. This apprehension causes the superior to have a lack of subordinate trust. This idea might not, however, be right, as, in many ways, there are more competent subordinates than their superiors.

d. Superior's preoccupation:

A superior believes that each and every matter needs to be conveyed to him since he is still concerned with his own job. The interaction of supervisors with their subordinates is a significant productivity criterion that many managers ignore as an excuse due to a lack of time.

e. Knowledge lack:

Inadequate knowledge of the meaning of communication and its utility in different ways may not be given the desired attention by superiors at times. This can contribute to minimal or inadequate information transmission affecting the organization. This can contribute to ineffectiveness and mismanagement.

f. Communicating with hesitation:

This appears to be a justification for subordinates to not engage with their superiors. Subordinates are unable to communicate such information to the superior, as such part of information can have a detrimental impact on them. The hesitation to communicate, therefore, takes place.

5. Mechanical Obstacles:

Another category of factors that hinder the smooth flow of communication is mechanical barriers.

There are:

a. Inadequate message transmission arrangement:

Proper coding and decoding facilities are included in the arrangements. This is usually carried out to control such machines by coding machines and qualified workers. When sensitive information is sent, top classified, confidential, etc., under various classifications, sufficient care must be taken in transmitting it. It should not be leaked to unauthorized individuals. Responsible personnel must manage the confidentiality and security of sensitive information.

b. Layout bad office:

A proper information center is an inescapable requirement for the transmission of messages inside and outside the organization. Different types of information, such as wireless sets, radio communication systems, electronic machines, FAX, e-mail, etc., are therefore needed. Infrastructural facilities are very important for efficient communication in order to accommodate these systems. There may be different barriers to the transmission of information in their absence.

c. Defective activities and procedures:

Procedures for the docketing of incoming and outgoing messages properly maintained in an information center must be established. Also, adequate arrangements for allocating priority messages such as urgent, most urgent, etc., and their subsequent transmissions would negate the very purpose of communicating if all of these are not investigated.

d. False medium use:

In mechanical contact, this is another obstacle. The sender of the message is responsible for selecting the correct medium. Let's take the sending of letters from one company to another in a distant location, for example.

Whether or not the letter should be sent by normal mail to Speed Post, Courier, FAX, or e-mail depends on the importance of the action to be taken at the end of the receipt. This element needs to be determined at all times by the sender himself. The sender must also choose a suitable communication medium.

6. Barriers to Status:

An organizational member's status is determined by the role he occupies in the organization. A middle-level manager can be too concerned about his senior and pay minimum attention to the thoughts of his subordinate. A sense of dynamic inferiority in the subordinate's mind doesn't encourage him to seek clarification from the superior. H. As follows, Kelly found few effects of status on communication:

Low status and high-status member: members with low ranks share more irrelevant information than members of high status. High-status individuals tend to be prohibited from expressing criticism, lower status negative attitudes towards their own work.

Communication with high-status individuals; thus, organizational interaction and communication are affected by the perceptions of rank and position.

Poor supervision- If a supervisor suspects or acts as a self-appointed censor or listens closely to his subordinates, the communication is blocked.

7. Perceptual obstacles:

Individual experience is one of the most common causes of the communication barrier. In view of his own background and ability, a person receiving a message may interpret it because there is a mutual distrust of misunderstanding between the sender and the receiver of the message. On the other hand, if there is openness in the relationship, it is easy to believe all that is shared.

8. Information filtering:

Filtering is the name of every effort to change and color details to present a more desirable impression. Only the information is passed on to their superiors by the subordinates, which would project them in a positive light that the superior needs to hear. When an employee is due for a promotion or pay raise, this distortion of contact becomes more serious.

9. Expertise:

And when they function side by side, it appears to divide people. Different roles can make individuals feel that they line indifferent worlds with special interests and job jargon. Sectional interest and departmental loyalty discourage workers from looking at organizational challenges from a wider viewpoint and from listening to the point of view of others.

10. The time pressure:

Managers under great time pressure, particularly those at higher work, cannot afford to engage and communicate regularly with their subordinates. Such time pressure can cause problems with communication between them.

11. Unclarified hypothesis:

The data found in the message is normally accompanied by some assumptions. The sender may have been explicit about the assumptions, but there is likely to be a case of inadequate contact, leading to various interpretations, unless they are communicated with the recipient. It is, therefore, essential for the communicator to illustrate the assumptions that underlie his message.

4.2 Steps to Overcome Barriers

The sender, recipient, and others try to overcome barriers to communication. What can people do to mitigate challenges and strive and resolve these obstacles, given that there are barriers to communication? In making communication more efficient, the following suggestions should be helpful:

A. Overcoming the barriers of the sender part:

1. Idea preparation and clarification: It is important that the ideas are planned and explained in mind before starting some kind of communication.

2. Differing expectations:

In order to resolve different perspectives, the message should be explained so that people with different views and experiences will understand it. We should know, if possible, the history of those with whom we are going to communicate. Empathizing and viewing the situation from the point of view of the other person and delaying responses before weighing the relevant data helps to minimize contradictory messages

3. Overcoming language differences:

The definitions of unconventional or technological words should be clarified to address language gaps. It is necessary to use simple, straightforward, natural language. In order to ensure that all-important concepts have been clarified, it is especially helpful to ask the recipient to clarify or restate the key points of the letter.

4. Overcoming verbal and non-verbal inconsistent communication:

The keys to removing contact contradictions are being aware of them and not attempting to send fake messages. The message should be settled on through movements, dress, stance, facial expression, and other powerful non-verbal communications. Non-verbal communication interpretation should agree with the post.

5. Emotionality overcoming:

Growing one's understanding of them is the first step in resolving the negative effects of emotionality. It is good to be sensitive to one's own moods and to be mindful of how they might affect others before delivering an important message to them. It is also helpful to try to understand the emotional responses of others and to brace oneself beforehand for coping with emotional experiences.

It is difficult to interact verbally with people with a high degree of emotionality. Before any discussion, it is, therefore, best to write them a memo or a letter. This approach can also be used to eliminate errors by people who can express themselves better in writing than in oral form.

B. Overcoming barriers on the receiver's part: overcoming prejudicial decision-

1. Focus on the Message, not the messenger:

Often, before we really understand the messages communicated by that person, we seem to have a preconceived opinion about others. We are very unlikely to listen to his message with total attention and magnanimity if we are prejudiced against a colleague.

Besides personal preference, by his manner and demeanor, his outward presence, facial expression, and even body language, we also judge our messenger. Because all of these could also influence our acceptance of his message, we should remind ourselves that the reason for contact is the message and not the messenger.

2. Overcoming poor listening:

Developing an active listening habit can help to significantly enhance communication. Focusing on what the purpose of the sender is, having the patience to listen to it until it ends without attempts to disturb it, and saving the mind from wandering away, will contribute to a greater understanding of the sender's message.

3. Be open-minded:

Second, consider what a person is trying to communicate, i.e., have an open mind to other ideas and suggestions, keeping all your notions aside.

C. Overcoming challenges in organization and others:

1. Noise obstacle overcoming:

Noise is any disturbance between the sender and the receiver that takes place. This is why any communication problem that cannot be adequately described as "noise" is normally detected. In order to overcome the noise barrier for successful communication, its source must be found. Maybe that's not easy. Noise happens in a number of ways, and it is also very subjective, which means that one form of noise that distracts a person does not distract the other person.

Have you ever been distracted by the images on the wall during a conversation, the view from the window, a paper lying open on a desk, or a conversation taking place in an adjacent room? A lot of individuals have been so busy. Have you ever been puzzled by irrelevant content or the illogical approach taken by the author in the study of written communication? Many people have, again.

Once the source or causes of the noise have been found, steps to resolve it can be taken. It is not always possible to overcome the noise barrier; however, luckily, only the knowledge of its presence by either the sender or the recipient of a message will help enhance the flow of communication.

2. Use of feedback:

Feedback is answered; without it, the message sender is unable to know whether the receiver has received the entire message or has grasped its intent. There is no information in a one-way relationship. Such communication includes forwarding ideas, details, directions, and orders through the chain of command from higher management without asking for an answer or checking to see if any action has taken place. It is not sufficient to make sure the message has been received.

The employer and superior should encourage input on their order or guidance. Feedback helps to correct and reinforce the correctness of what is incorrect. Moreover, grievances, rumors, and reasons for not being able to deliver promises are also eradicated.

Therefore, a two-way mechanism must occur for communication to be successful so that the sender knows if the message has been understood. The two-way communication system involves sending a message down the command chain and sending back up the chain a response containing data, ideas, and feelings.

3. Organizational structure simplification:

A basic structure of the company that does not use multiple layers in a communication chain helps to keep the information exchanged quicker, and there are fewer chances of message loss during transmission.

4. Selecting the right media:

By using various platforms, a message can be transmitted. Choosing the correct type of media based on the type and intent of the message and the level of individuals to which the message is intended can help to resolve the challenges created by the selection of incorrect media.

Those are some of the general suggestions; we should use them to resolve communication barriers. In order to minimize communication hurdles, the following steps can be taken:

Step-1. The managers within the company must plan and follow an open door contact policy.

Step-2. In order to fill the capacity gap, they can also build an environment of faith and trust in the organization.

Step-Three. No manager may receive a creditability passport unless the details stated by him are well known and acknowledged by the individuals concerned. The purpose of the communication policy should be:

1. Two-way communication promotion:

There should not be void in contact. That means that communication should flow downward and upward in both directions. It is important to provide a sound feedback system in order to prevent confusion and distortion of messages.

2. Strengthening of the communication network:

In order to strengthen the communication network, the communication procedure should be streamlined; downstream communication layers should be reduced to the minimum possible level, decentralization and delegation of authority should be reduced in order to make informal communication less necessary by means of regular meetings, conferences and timely distribution of information to subordinates.

3. The message should be oriented towards the listener:

For the audience, the message must be of interest. It should be simple, complete, succinct, precise, and right so that the receiver can receive it and interpret it in the same way.

4. Suitable contact medium must be chosen:

The communication medium should be chosen in such a way that, in time, the message reaches its destination, to the right person, and in the context in which it was framed. The persuasion model of communication from Hove Land can assist policymakers in this regard.

5. Eliminating organizational barriers:

Communication challenges should be avoided to the fullest extent possible. Knowledge filtering or spinning, bossism, and consciousness of position do not come in the way of contact. Other obstacles should be eliminated to the extent possible, such as physical or socio-psychological or semantic ones.

6. Promoting participatory approach:

A participatory approach to management should be encouraged by management. Sub-ordinates should be invited to take part in the process of decision-making. It will pursue collaboration and decrease many barriers to communication.

Therefore, in order to facilitate the coherence between sub-ordinations, a well-defined, open door communication policy covering all the points should be followed in the organization.

- **Overcoming communication barriers-In an organization (with measures)**

Given the importance of good communication in the efficient functioning of business organizations, overcoming these obstacles is necessary on the part of management. Although these obstacles cannot be entirely eliminated, effective managerial efforts in this direction will mitigate the impact of these obstacles to the degree that adequate and objective knowledge flows in various directions. It is possible to take the following steps in this regard:

1. Organizational strategy must be transparent and concise and promote the flow of information so that people at all levels understand the full meaning of communication. It is important. In explicit and unambiguous terms, the organizational policy should convey that the organization favors the promotion of contact in the organization.

2. The subject matter to be communicated should also be defined by this regulation. This does not suggest that

communication material should be prescribed in a fully exclusive way, but that the list should be illustrative, and it should emphasize that the organization's needs should decide the subject matter of communication.

3. Although communication through the right channel is crucial for the orderly flow of information, it should not always be emphasized. As far as routine forms of information are related, the mechanism of communication through the correct channel serves the purpose appropriately. However, this must be ignored were and whatever the situation so warrants, and it must be specifically told to those concerned that insistence on the proper channel is not appropriate in all situations.

4. The duty for effective communication is shared by every person in the organization, but in this regard, individuals at the top have a special responsibility. Only if top management is adamant that it is to be so will a good communication mechanism be accomplished. It must set good examples on its own, explicitly expect others to follow them, and check that there are no bottlenecks from time to time.

5. For the promotion of contact, organizations should have sufficient facilities. The adequate provision of such facilities is not adequate, but due consideration must be paid to their proper and efficient use. These need to be closely studied, and the duty of superior administrators to promote the use of these facilities is reinforced by the introduction of supportive behaviors and behavioral needs.

6. As communication is an interpersonal method, its promotion requires the establishment of interpersonal relationships based on mutual respect, confidence, and trust. Status differentials and class distinctions are overemphasized in large companies, rendering interpersonal relationships between executives extremely impersonal and formal.

Therefore, to make it more intimate and personal, the organizational environment should be dramatically changed. For the promotion of communication, a shift in the attitude and actions of individuals is necessary. To this end, an instructional contact curriculum for managers at all levels should be coordinated. Managers should be advised in this program on the need and importance of communication, the need to establish close personal connections between people.

7. The software for analyzing the flow of communication in various directions should be a continuous one. This would illustrate problems recognizing their triggers in this field and thus encourage the implementation of effective corrective measures.

1. Get officially confirmed:

If a director doesn't know or understand, he can't talk. A manager must also learn and appreciate the knowledge that he is supposed to convey clearly. Normally, he should be able to answer any questions that the subordinates present. His knowledge and comprehension span should be greater than his contact span with his workers.

2. Plainness:

In order for the message to be interpreted by the receiver, messages should be designed in straightforward and plain language.

3. Consistency:

Messages have to be compatible with each other. Orders should be aligned with the organization's known goals and with its other operations.

4. Suitability:

In communication, the objective is to ensure an efficient flow of data. It would be enough to cover the fields, but where instructions are difficult, they should not be smothered; they should be repeated, probably in different ways.

5. Timing and punctuality:

Different people and groups at the same time or the same individuals and groups at different times will receive or respond to the same message differently. The situational, psychological, and technological aspects of timing are discussed by effective communication. A delayed report ceases to be a monitoring medium with respect to timeliness and becomes a historical text.

6. Distribution:

The failure of information to reach the correct position or person is one of the most frequent causes of performance deficiencies. It is often as important to who is to be told as to what is to be told. The recipient of a message should be aware of its purpose, e.g., for action, information, or another purpose. A top-to-bottom interaction should move through every stage of the authority line.

7. Balance between uniformity and adaptability:

An organization's smooth operation depends in part on its uniformity. Yet, when different situations and individuals are involved, adaptability should be resorted to. Orders and reports may be communicated by means of systems which provide opportunities to adapt to unique situations.

8. Interest and acceptation:

The goal of the interaction is to secure a positive reaction. The person referred to should be interested in the message and accept it. Downward communication is more effective if morale is strong, and when the superior is a good listener, upward communication gets through.

It is, therefore, necessary for the manager to cultivate a positive attitude towards communication. He must ensure that the subordinates are adequately trained and that they feel trained. The manager should also gain others' trust; when the receiver understands the intent of the communicator, the meaning is more effectively imported. In addition, a manager must use the informal organization as a communication medium, as the most efficient communication occurs when managers use the informal organization to complement the formal organization's communication channels.

9. Similarity maintaining:

People of various cultural backgrounds who work in an organization vary from each other. The presence of differences is often desirable to assume before similarity is known. Individuals still believe that others are like them. Until similarity is proven, the sound theory is to presume the existence of differences.

10. Emphasize specification:

Instead of explanation or assessment, another important rule is to emphasize definition. It is advisable that the decision is postponed until the observation and analysis of the situation are completed from the different viewpoints of all the cultures concerned.

11. Hypothesis for working:

The understanding of cross-cultural communication is viewed as a theory that requires prior testing to enhance cross-cultural communication.

12. Patient's:

Working in an intercultural setting is rather a challenging and stressful activity, as a contact in such an organization may be tiresome, actions may be unacceptable, and things may not get as expected. In such situations, patience with yourself and others will help overcome conflicts and prevent them from occurring in the future.

13. Empathy:

Empathy in any relationship, where a certain degree of depth of understanding is required, can be hailed as the primary prerequisite for a satisfactory experience. Empathy is independent of sympathy. Empathy is feeling, not feeling sorry for the other person, which is compassion.

Before sending a message, the sender of the message should put himself/herself in the shoes of the receiver. He / She needs to know the recipient's principles, background, and frame of reference. He / She needs to see the other person as he/she is and recognize them.

14. Questions to ask:

If there is something, we don't understand or want to know why someone has acted in a certain way, just inquire. Asking questions prevents us from making assumptions and helps to build our intercultural information bank.

15. Term of writing:

It is commonly shown that individuals who do not have English as their mother tongue can read more skillfully than they write. It is a safe idea to write stuff down as a back-up at all times.

16. Positive:

Steer away from responsibility and confrontation when faced with events of an intercultural nature. To ensure flawlessness, remain optimistic and evaluate the problem sports and function as a team to frame tactics and solutions.

17. Self-reflect:

Not only external but also inward, a strong intercultural communicator assesses. Take time to focus on the style of communication, management, or motivation to see whereas a person you can develop.

18. Value:

Respect is the backbone of all intercultural contact. We gain respect and help to build more open and harmonious relationships by showing respect.

29. Overcome prejudices:

Miscommunication should be resolved by concentrating on the message and not the messenger due to pre-defined ideas regarding the sender. He does have a negative attitude about any contact with Y if X does not like Y. To make communication efficient, personal biases and prejudices should be avoided.

Chapter 5: Effective Communication Means Business Success

For any business owner, effective communication is a vital tool. The difference between sealing a deal and missing out on a potential opportunity can be your success at getting your point across.

You should be able to explain business policies clearly to customers and clients and to answer their customers' questions or services. In order To make sure you reach your goals, it is crucial to communicate effectively in negotiations.

Communication within the company is also important. Effective communication can help promote a good working relationship between you and your workers, which can raise morale and effectiveness in turn.

The main aspects of both verbal and non-verbal communication, how to interpret and understand others and how to give the people you meet in and around your company the best possible first impression.

5.1 Communication is Crucial for A Successful Business

Effective business communication is important for any company to thrive and develop. Company communication is often goal-oriented, unlike ordinary communication. Yet, research shows that 60% of professionals in internal communications do not calculate internal communications.

Corporations with large numbers of individuals and varying levels of hierarchy also fail to efficiently manage business communication. Therefore, in an organization, between organizations and society at large, there should be efficient and continuing contact between supervisors and subordinates.

1. Enhances engagement of employees

Ragan's research on employee engagement demonstrates that the top internal communication factor that statistically correlates to how engaged employees are in leadership communication. In supporting, coaching, and reminding leaders of the significance of communication, internal communication teams have an important role.

2. Eliminates overload emails

Email is used within businesses for everything from information requests, employee communication and feedback, status reports, task assignments, customer and supplier communications, meeting invites, distribution of documents, HR notices on different team activities, benefits, and birthday wishes.

- **Enterprise-communications-emails**

Eradicate reported that 25 percent of the workday is spent by the average corporate worker on different email-related tasks.

Only a tiny fraction of the emails that hit our inbox, however, deserve our immediate attention by the sender or sub-filter out the important emails. In addition, many emails that we receive are not at all relevant to us.

This issue of email overload has been eliminated by internal business communications technical technology methods for employee engagement and communication.

3. Eliminates silos of communication

Too much content that is irrelevant often results in information silos. In other words, data that is actually important in the workplace can easily get lost. Ask yourself why the information in the organization gets lost.

To eliminate this challenge, proper internal business communications and the use of the right communications tools are crucial.

4. Increases productivity for workers

4 in 5 employees believe that their job performance is helped by effective internal business communications.

With the overload of information, staff often spend too much information searching for content they need to do their job.

In addition, an average worker spends 2.5 hours every day searching for needed information. This results in a monthly loss of time throughout the week to find something that should be at the fingertips of workers.

All managers want their teams to be inspired and help employees improve their productivity, but you may sometimes wonder how to get there. Fortunately, enhancing your internal communication has a dominant effect on the motivation and productivity of your staff.

Whether you are considering implementing a new internal communication channel in your business or are interested in further optimizing the dynamics you already have in place, these efforts are likely to improve the productivity of your employees.

Here are five ways in which effective internal communication can increase workplace productivity for employees:

a. Great internal communication that saves time for your employees

If you've optimized the internal communication patterns of your team, it means that when they need it, everyone has easy access to all the information they need. Every day, the typical knowledge worker loses an average of 2.5 hours of working time hunting for the resources needed.

Think about it: that's more than a quarter of people's time spent just looking for the data they require to do their jobs on an average working day of about eight hours!

It's a given that when you get the right information at the right moment, your employees are more productive, so that they can spend those hours doing their job rather than making a call, waiting for one of their colleagues to respond to an email, or running searches to find the right file. You have to arm them with all the resources they need to get their jobs done if you desire to improve the productivity of your employees. Effective internal communication is the key to productivity for employees.

b. Effective internal communication can raise the commitment of employees

Improved internal communication contributes directly to a healthier working atmosphere and greater involvement of workers, and enterprises with a highly engaged workforce are 22% more successful. The link that employees feel with your company, its values, and its different projects is enhanced by good communication across all management levels.

Staff sees that their contributions are valued when knowledge flows as it should and feel inspired to be as effective as possible. What's more, when the workers truly understand the intent of their ventures, they will feel more involved in the success of your company and will be more likely to remain in the company.

c. Internal coordination is essential to the successful management of projects

A perfect way to prevent misunderstandings and clear up uncertainty is to have an efficient internal communication strategy in place. Think about it: they know exactly what is expected from them when the workers receive straightforward project orders, direct feedback, and unambiguous deadlines.

Good internal communication helps workers perform on the assigned assignments and tasks and saves time that a confused worker working on the wrong assignment might waste.

d. Awesome internal communication enhances workplace trust and collaboration

It creates an environment of confidence and mutual support in which innovation and productivity flourish when the business enjoys transparent, free-flowing contact across all departments and between all employees.

Bad communication, on the other hand, causes mistrust and resentment in the workplace where workers waste time observing the work of each other and avoid delegating and sharing duties. The best antidote to micromanaging is good internal communication. This motivates workers to feel confident to take on responsibility and succeed.

What's more, they can quickly recognize and fill knowledge gaps, cultivate a learning culture, and improve team productivity when workers are encouraged to share their best practices and key lessons with their colleagues.

e. Open collaboration helps to create a better atmosphere for work

It is also said that "information is power." You share the knowledge that empowers your staff when you foster a culture of open and clear communication in your business. This includes taking the extra time to clarify a project's overall intent, how a report affects the organization, or why you're undertaking the research, but you'll find it's time well spent.

Employees who understand not only what they do but also why they do it in a particular way treat their job. They think about the task's overall success and don't simply want to cross the project off their to-do list.

5. Enhances cross-departmental coordination

It is very difficult to maintain successful interdepartmental organizations within organizations without a proper communications strategy. They have to be able to join and interact effectively in order for jobs to be more efficient.

For example, your research department has to be on the same page as your marketing team, and your office administration has to be in touch with the IT department. Business-communication-collaboration

6. Enhances interaction with remote employees

Remote teams are the job's future. More than 40 percent of the world's working population will be mobile by 2022, the Global Mobile Workforce Forecast Update has estimated. In addition, the figures could soon reach 75 percent in developed countries such as the US.

This implies that a new kind of approach to communication, leadership, and management is required. Only a few communication challenges that remote teams face are coordinating across time zones, data silos, and overcoming language and cultural barriers. Moreover, distance often makes it more difficult for team members to feel like a team.

Better internal business communications can have a major positive impact on how remote teams work together and feel.

7. Reduces turnover for employees

Companies with more committed and satisfied workers enjoy significantly lower turnover rates. Managers have to make sure to keep their staff informed about what is relevant to their jobs in order to attract and keep Millennials and younger generations in the workplace.

On the other hand, too much irrelevant data often leads to stress, disengagement, frustration, and, with that, reduced retention of employees.

8. Improves efforts at knowledge sharing

One of the main objectives companies is trying to achieve by investing in internal communications practices hence best practices in the sharing of knowledge.

Employers need to allow easy sharing of knowledge in their organizations in a world where employees are constantly growing and learning new things.

Organizational knowledge suffers without a well-set internal business communications strategy.

9. Increases advocacy for workers

They are even more active in making their employees into brand ambassadors when managers know how to interact effectively with their employees.

As many businesses claim, brand ambassadorship is not so difficult to achieve. Happy staff would actually love to contribute to brand ambassadorship schemes.

There are key ways in which brand ambassadorship and employee advocacy will benefit the activities of the company:

Increase recognition of brands

Enhance the reputation of the employer and attract high-quality marketing endeavors

Enhance revenue

10. Improves the satisfaction and retention of customers

Better business contact also means better satisfaction for customers. Two things happen when it comes to clients' satisfaction and service if there is an insufficient combination in an organization.

Next, workers in customer-facing positions won't have the data they need. Second, clients can feel the low morale of workers and have a negative experience.

In fact, one study showed that the attitude of employees has a substantial effect on customer satisfaction, resulting in a sales increase.

11. Constructs a stronger atmosphere of business

Finally, for creating a better organizational climate, a proper corporate relations plan is essential.

Companies that interact in a straightforward and open manner provide a far healthier work climate, enthusiasm for workers, and satisfaction.

On the other hand, companies that ignore business communications as a way of enhancing the culture of the workforce suffer from low commitment, high turnover rates, and low satisfaction rates for workers and customers.

Conclusion

Normally, the term communication refers to the exchange of information and thoughts about their needs, aspirations, or perceptions between two individuals or business organizations, in words, actions, or symbols, provided that the content for the recipient and sender must mean the same. Communications in non-linguistic or oral forms may be of a local or international flavor, in spoken or alternative modes, and depend on conformist or unconventional signals.

In business, communication is a channel that, with the sole purpose of closing a sale, helps to promote a service, product, or organization. For communication, companies use a variety of media, including radio, outdoor advertising, and television, print, the Internet, and even word of mouth. In terms of business etiquette and interpersonal skills, advanced communication skills have achieved an exalted status, and employees and managers in each organization honor their communication skills for better mutual understanding and engagement, not only for internal purposes but also for outside stakeholders. Providentially, the business environment provides the senders and receivers of messages with a range of communication modes to satisfy their communication needs.

Some of the results of effective communication are that it helps companies to keep the company healthy, maximizes their profits, and not only keeps their employees engaged and happy but also helps them to concentrate sufficiently on their job to achieve the goals of the company.

Communication is the cornerstone of an organization, and without it, an organization would cease to exist.

Its main functions are the exchange of information and options, the drafting of proposals, plans, and agreements, the execution of decisions, the transmission or fulfillment of orders, and, in general, the execution of sales. Organizational activity is an organization's bloodstream, and when communication falters, all activities end.

In a company, there are two forms of business communication, which come under vertical communication, internal and external. Internal communication is all communication that has to do with internal matters and interaction between employers and employees in different ways. And it acts as an exemplary means to resolve all employee grievances, thereby improving aspects of goodwill, work satisfaction, efficiency, and protection. This also helps to raise turnover and income.

You have, under internal communication, upwards, downward, and horizontal / Lateral. External communication refers to communication with organizations outside the organization, for example, with clients and suppliers, by company supervisors. This type of contact and helpful engagement will contribute to operational productivity, business reputation, goodwill, corporate image, customer loyalty, organizational objectives, resulting in success, and increased volumes of sales, followed by a strong showing of profit.

The communication process includes the message, encoding, decoding, medium, and feedback. There are different kinds of barriers that affect the process. These barriers can overcome by using simple strategies. Effective communication is a key element in the success of a business. It improves employee motivation, customer satisfaction, which leads to an increase in product sales and quality, which helps in achieving company goals.

This is not a onetime process. It is a continuous process. It should be regularly evaluated by management for improvements.

Printed in Great Britain
by Amazon

83817167R00068